The American Artisan

CHRISTOFFER PETERSEN

The American Artisan

By Christoffer Petersen

Copyright © Christoffer Petersen, 2022

AARLUUK PRESS

Christoffer Petersen has asserted his right under the Copyright, Designs and Patents Act 1988 to be identified as the author of this work.

ISBN: 978-87-94119-60-3

www.christoffer-petersen.com

Glossary of West Greenlandic Words

aap – yes
ana – grandmother
anaana – mother
angakkoq – shaman
ata – grandfather
ataata – father
eeqqi – no (East Greenland)
iiji – yes (East Greenland)
imaqa – maybe
naamik – no
kaffemik – celebration/party
kamikker/kamiks – sealskin boots
mattak – whale skin and blubber delicacy
qajaq – kayak
qujanaq – thank you
tuttu – reindeer
ukaleq – Arctic hare

Introduction

The American Artisan is the twenty-third novella to feature Constable David Maratse. I have always enjoyed writing a *Maratse* novella as I feel as though I get to explore ideas and plots that either don't fit or don't work in the novels or other series. A *Maratse* novella is usually short, between 60 and 80 paperback pages long. But what I think binds them together is a Jack Londonesque – my definition – setting, plot or theme. There is often a chase sequence, be it with boats, dogs and sledges, or maybe on foot. But all the novellas are firmly placed in the harsh, unforgiving outdoors. If that's your kind of read, then you're in luck, especially as I have plenty more in the works.

This novella was written as a Kickstarter reward, and introduces the character of David 'Dave' Bennett. If you like the idea of starring alongside Maratse or other characters from my different series, then be sure to keep an eye on my website for news of upcoming Kickstarter campaigns.

The American Artisan is shamelessly linked to *Northern Mail*, an earlier novella in the same series.

Chris
March 2022
Denmark

Part 1

It was a quiet convention. A chill wind pressed upon the thick panes of glass stretching from just above the floor and halfway up the walls of the modern gallery with the wave-formed roof – inspired by the Northern Lights that graced the sky during Nuuk's darker months. Guests mingled in the foyer of *Katuaq*, Nuuk's cultural centre, bumping elbows as they pressed in groups around small tables tucked into the walls of the centre, ringing the auditorium at the heart of the building. The auditorium was the prize, for sure, with keynote speakers bringing the rich history of Greenland's stamps to life, but it was at the smaller artist's tables that real treasure might be found.

Dave Bennett bumped through the throng of guests from one artisan's table to the next like a ball in a pinball machine. He carried a small satchel over one shoulder, tucking it into his six-foot frame and apologising his way through the crowd as he made his way to a small table that had caught his eye. A ring of short but engaged Greenlanders blocked his path, and he took a moment to look at the framed prints on the wall, adjusting his grey-brown hair after a glimpse of it in the glass, before squeezing into the gap recently vacated by an older Greenlandic man. Dave reached the table, glanced at the postcard-sized cachets preserved in sleeves of plastic, before bending over the table to inspect them.

"All genuine," said the woman sitting at the table. "All original." She lifted one, turned it over to show the back side, and smiled. "All signed," she said.

"So I see."

Dave looked up to catch the woman's eye, caught the splinter of light that flashed in her brown eyes as she smiled. The crease of her thin lips revealed a lifetime of smiles ingrained in her dark, wrinkled face.

"This one," she said, pressing the cachet into Dave's hands, "is by an American artist."

Dave nodded as he took the cachet. He smiled as the woman described the playful scene of polar bears and seals lounging about on the ice floe to which a set of stamps from 1982 had been applied.

"Very popular," the woman said, continuing with her accented English. "You should buy it before somebody else does."

"I might," Dave said, adding, "I did wonder what had become of it."

He reached inside his jacket for the name tag hanging from his neck, then held it up beside the signature on the cachet. Dave smiled as the woman leaned over the table to read both names – the printed one and the signature scrawled beside it.

"Yep," Dave said as the woman reached out to tug the name tag for a closer look. He dipped his head as she pulled the tag, then steadied himself with a hand on the table as the woman frowned.

"*You're* the artist?"

"Yes." Dave straightened his back as the woman let go of his name tag. He placed the cachet on the table and reached out to shake the woman's hand. "David Bennett," he said. "Please call me, Dave."

"Qilaatti Upperneq," she said.

The woman gripped Dave's hands, grinning as she held his gaze.

"And what do I call you?" Dave asked.

"Qilaatti Upperneq."

"Okay, Qila…"

"…tti," she said.

Another guest, an old man with a shock of thick grey hair, squeezed through a gap between tables as Qilaatti let go of Dave's hands. He swapped a few words with Qilaatti in Greenlandic, then turned to look at Dave as Qilaatti pointed at him. The man continued in Greenlandic, pausing every sixth or seventh word for Qilaatti to translate, ignoring her sighs and soft slaps on his arm when she told him to slow down.

"He wants your signature," Qilaatti said.

"My signature?"

"Autograph," the man said. He patted his jacket pockets, searching for a slip of paper. Qilaatti pressed a blank postcard into his hand, holding onto the corner when he tried to tug it free.

"One hundred kroner," she said.

Dave watched the man pull out his wallet, then waved the money away. "That's not necessary," he said. Qilaatti took the money, gave Dave her pen, then set about tidying the cachets from her stall into a soft leather wallet as Dave signed the postcard.

She tucked the wallet into a sealskin satchel, nodded at the man as Dave made a quick sketch beside his autograph, and then plucked another hundred kroner from the man's wallet. When Dave protested, she took his arm, whisking him away from the table the second Dave gave the man the postcard.

"I'm buying you a coffee," she said, leading Dave through the crowd. "This is Greenland. Coffee is expensive." Then, as she took his hand, she said, "Come with me."

Qilaatti was even shorter when she stood than when she sat on the stool at her table. She chattered to Dave as she guided him through the convention's guests to the café at the far end of *Katuaq*. They found a table. Qilaatti pressed her satchel into Dave's hands and left him to *make camp* as she called it, before twisting her way around the café guests to order at the counter. Dave caught his breath, sat down, and *made camp*.

The warm air inside the centre blistered with snippets of conversation – German here, English there, some Danish, a lot of Greenlandic, and the occasional burst of Chinese. Dave hung his jacket on the back of his chair, then stood up to greet Qilaatti as she returned to the table with two large hot chocolates overflowing with whipped cream, sprinkled with dark chocolate.

"We can have a coffee once we have finished these," she said. "We have much to talk about."

"Of course," Dave said. He reached for the spoon resting on the saucer, patted his belly and promised himself that *one was fine* and that it was lunchtime after all.

"So," Qilaatti said. "You are the American artisan."

"I'm the *what*?"

"The artist," she said, with a nod at her satchel. "I have collected lots of your work. People like the carica…" She paused to suck her teeth, as if resetting her mouth before trying again. "Caricatures of the animals."

"Yes," Dave said. "They're fun to draw."

"Even more fun to sell," Qilaatti said. She looked over her shoulder, noticed the man who bought Dave's autograph at a table close to the café, and then muttered something about *following up on a sale*. "I'm not a collector," she said as her brow wrinkled. "I'm a businesswoman. I'm in it for the money."

"You're in the stamp business," Dave said, nodding.

"*Aap*." Qilaatti pointed at her satchel hanging over the back of the chair between them. "On a good day I can sell for a few thousand kroners. But," she said, shrugging her shoulders. "On the same day I will use a few thousand kroners – maybe a little more – buying more cachets, more stamps, extra sleeves…" Qilaatti shook her head, stopping herself before the list continued. "I sell everything I buy, but today," she said as she dipped her spoon into the whipped cream melting into her chocolate. "Today is the first day I have made a profit."

"And you just spent it on me," Dave said. He reached into his jacket, searching for his wallet. "Here," he said, pulling out a two hundred kroner note. "Let me pay."

"*Naamik*," Qilaatti said. "Put your money away. This is my treat."

Qilaatti steered the conversation, putting Dave at ease as she quizzed him about his journey to Greenland, his love of stamps, his art, his work, and his family, including his lovely wife, Jill, and their three fabulous nieces.

"But this is your first time in Nuuk?" she asked.

"First time in Greenland," he said.

Qilaatti's thin lips spread in a wide smile. She brushed a wayward length of black hair from her fringe – jet black despite her age – and then opened her mouth to speak. She stopped short of asking more questions; the words clinging to her lips as her eyes glimpsed something behind Dave. He turned, caught the eye of a thin Greenlandic man about half his age, and then froze as the man stared at him and sneered.

"Look at me," Qilaatti said, reaching for Dave's hand. She patted his wrist. "Mr Bennett?"

"Yes?" Dave said, pulling away from the man's stare. "Who's that?"

"Trouble," Qilaatti said. "Don't look at him. Don't speak to him."

"Why?"

Qilaatti shook her head. "Best you don't know."

She took over the conversation as Dave fell silent. Something about the man's stare, his brown, almost black eyes, and the white scar on his chin left him with a queasy feeling in his stomach that had nothing to do with the rich cream and sugary chocolate. The man had a penetrating stare that

Dave struggled to think he could ever forget. It was his first and only xenophobic experience since arriving in Greenland. And yet, it was more unsettling than that; the man's hostility was tempered with something worse. There were flecks of interest in the man's eyes that seemed to spark as he stared at Dave, almost as if a solution to a problem had suddenly presented itself.

"Mr Bennett," Qilaatti said, pulling Dave back into the conversation with another pat of his wrist.

"Yes," he said. "I'm sorry." He smiled and said, "What were we talking about?"

"Your work," she said. Qilaatti's eyes shone as she added, "And more of those doodles."

"Doodles?"

Qilaatti reached for her satchel, opened the front flap, and pulled out a stack of black postcards. "Doodles and your name," she said, sliding the postcards across the table. "Five will get you lunch. If you make ten, we can go out for dinner. Tonight," she said. "I will pick you up at your hotel." Qilaatti grinned. "What?" She said. "Do you have better plans?"

Dave recovered, fixed his glasses, and said, "I have no plans."

"Good. Then we will have dinner, and I will be your guide around Nuuk."

"I'd like that," Dave said. He looked up as Qilaatti glanced around him, but resisted the temptation to turn. He guessed the man was still watching him, and that Qilaatti – his newfound guide – had taken him under her wing and not just for profit, but for protection.

"Get scribbling," she said, placing a pen on the stack of postcards. "I'll find some customers."

Dave watched Qilaatti work her magic with the guests, pointing in his direction, drawing nods, smiles, and waves as he worked. Dave resisted the urge to pinch himself but couldn't help smiling as he wondered what Jill would say when he told of his new *rock star* status.

"Just imagine," he whispered, adding a wing of feathers to the goose he drew on the first postcard. "My first trip to Greenland…"

The thought burred inside Dave's head as he worked through the postcards. He tapped them into a neat stack, chiding himself for exploiting guests, until he remembered the pleasure on the man's face when he bought Dave's first autograph. Dave recognised the enthusiasm – one collector to another – and found some solace in the thought that the man might sell Dave's postcard, and it wasn't exploitation as such, but the beginning of a chain from one collector to another.

Dave let the thought twist away, preferring not to think of himself like that. Sure, he was an artist, but he was used to commissions. Doodling on Qilaatti's postcards made him think of selling art on the sidewalk, which took him back a few years – *many* years. Back then, he'd sell a few pieces, then grab a burger. Some forty years later, he was doing the same thing, halfway around the world.

It felt good.

It made him feel young.

And thoughts of the Greenlandic man with the scarred chin disappeared, along with the postcards, as Qilaatti brought a small group of collectors to their table.

Three coffees later, Dave left *Katuaq* with a pocketful of memories and a string of stories to tell Jill once he got back to his room. He scuffed the soles of his leather shoes in the sand and gravel sidewalks before stepping onto a paved pedestrian street that Qilaatti assured him was a prettier route back to the hotel. Dave paused at a shop window, fiddling with his glasses as he read the price tags on the souvenirs, the sealskin bags, and the impressive sealskin jacket in the window. It wasn't something he would buy, but as an artist, he couldn't ignore such excellent handiwork.

Just as he couldn't ignore the strong grip of the man who took his arm and pulled him into the narrow gap between two shops.

"You're going to help me," the man said in English. "You're going to be useful. Understand?"

Dave nodded, but words failed him, as he noticed the scar on the man's chin – a thick scar from a deep, ugly wound.

"Yes," Dave said when the man shook him. "I'll help you."

Part 2

North of Nuuk, on the sea ice, three kilometres south of Uummannaq Island, Constable David Maratse puffed on a cigarette clamped between his lips as he worked on a stubborn knot at the end of a long length of thick fishing line. The line was black, but brown oil seeped out of the weave and into the whorls on the skin of Maratse's fingers. He picked at the knot around the rusted ring of an old and heavy fishing lure. The wind brushed surface snow across Maratse's boots, piling in small drifts on the inside as the tops of the drifts smoked across the ice. Maratse turned slightly, then tugged the collars of his dirty police jacket a little higher to protect his neck from the chill fingers stretching across the frozen fjord. He squinted up at the bright sky, then lowered his gaze as he caught a smoky cackle from the old woman sitting cross-legged on the reindeer skins stretched across a weather-beaten sledge. Maratse smiled as the woman winked at him, nodded when she dipped her head to gesture at the knot, then shuffled again as the wind twisted tighter around his body.

"You've been working on that knot for twenty minutes," the woman said.

"Hmm."

Maratse concentrated. He wished, not for the first time, that his nails were just a little longer, or that Seeri Asasaq, the old woman on the sledge, would turn away so that he might use his knife.

"A bet is a bet, Constable," she said, cackling once more, as the knot confounded Maratse's best efforts to untie it. "You can start as soon as you like, or next weekend, perhaps. Whenever you're free."

Maratse lifted his head to look at the old woman. The lines on her face reminded him of a map, tracing the adventures of her life with deep contours across sun-browned cheeks. The lines around her eyes and mouth brought a smile to Maratse's lips as he imagined Seeri laughing long and hard around the campfire each summer, or when sitting close to the potbellied stove in a canvas wall tent, beating back the winter chill with long stories and strong coffee. Seeri carried the light of a hunter in her eyes, and when she looked at Maratse, he felt giddy with the memory of long sledge journeys across the ice, steep climbs to reindeer pastures, and the crack and boom of calving glaciers. Seeri Asasaq had lived a full life, but even as her body failed, the light shone still. Her fingers weren't as strong as they used to be, couldn't pick a knot, or even grasp a knife. But her mind was still as sharp as flint – sharp enough to tease Maratse into her debt with an impossible knot.

Seeri knew the young police constable would never untie it, just as Maratse knew he would do whatever she asked, regardless of the outcome of the bet. They both did. But it was the quiet understanding that drew them to each other – one hunter to another, each with a host of long stories perfect for dark winter evenings when the wind howled, and the snow scratched the windowpanes like sand in a desert storm. But Seeri's time for stories was running out, which led Maratse onto the ice on his day off, driving Seeri's small team of sledge dogs one more time, to her favourite spot on the fjord, to her favourite fishing hole.

"You're not married, Constable," she said, beckoning for Maratse to join her on the sledge.

"Neither are you," he said as he sat down. The sledge creaked as it moved under his weight and the dogs stirred, lifting their heads until Seeri gave a soft whistle for them to settle once more.

"I never saw the need," Seeri said. "I had a few friends." She dipped her head to one side, then reached out to pluck the cigarette from Maratse's mouth. She winked at him, took a long drag on the cigarette, then handed it back. The thin wind curled the smoke from her lips as she smiled. "I had some fun, back when I was younger." Seeri pursed her wrinkled lips as she thought about it. "But there was an urgency about them – those men."

"Your friends," Maratse said, finishing the cigarette.

"*Aap.*" Seeri nodded. She pressed a bare hand against her chest, tickling the hairs of her sealskin smock with short fingernails as she talked. "They were unsettled. Too intense." She reached for Maratse's hand, clasped it, and smiled. "You have a patience about you, Constable. If I was thirty years younger…"

"Hmm," Maratse said. He stretched his arm as Seeri pulled his hand into her lap. They looked out across the fjord, scanning the ice stretching to the Nuussuaq Peninsula, the shadowed slopes reaching down to the frozen sea, snow tails curling from the mountain peaks.

Seeri saw it first, squeezing Maratse's hand as she spotted a dark shape, no bigger than a football, pressing up out of the ice.

"Leave it," Seeri said, as Maratse reached for the saloon rifle tucked under a sealskin cord on the sledge. "I have plenty of meat."

Maratse let go of the rifle, and they watched the seal in silence.

"You never answered my question, Constable," Seeri said, once the seal was gone. "Why aren't you married?"

Maratse shrugged, then gestured at the icebergs locked into the frozen sea and the mountains in the distance. "No time," he said.

Seeri laughed, then patted Maratse's hand.

"Then find time, *Constable*, before it's too late."

She pushed him away and Maratse stood up. The dogs stirred. Seeri clicked her tongue, and they stood, shaking the windblown snow from their flanks before padding across the ice to the sledge. A large male with thick brown fur, black eyes, and a bald, pink nose pressed his face into Seeri's chest. She dug her fingers into his fur. The dog's ear trembled as Seeri pressed her lips close and whispered into it. Maratse watched for a moment, then wrangled the remaining dogs – five fit and healthy sledge dogs with a touch of grey about their muzzles, just like the streaks of grey in Seeri's hair.

Maratse straightened the dogs' harnesses, nodding as he appraised each dog, wondering how often he would be able to look after them, and what he would do with them once Seeri was gone, or when his contract ended. He glanced at the old woman, caught her eye, and smiled as he wondered if she had been thinking the same thing.

"I have a brother," she said, pushing the wheel dog away and patting its rump as Maratse called to it. "His son will take them." She nodded at the dogs. "He'll be here at the end of the month. He'll take them then." Seeri pointed to the northeast, adding, "He's from Ukkusissat."

Maratse nodded. The ice, he knew, was good as far as Ukkusissat. But while the dogs were close to retirement, the wheel dog's genes would bring new blood to the settlement's dogs.

"If you can look after them until then?" Seeri asked.

"*Iiji*," Maratse said. He was about to add more, but as the dogs fidgeted, he lifted his head to stare at an approaching vehicle – dark blue, with a flash of white stripes on the side.

"That'll be for you," Seeri said.

Maratse straightened his back as the police patrol car drew nearer. The heavy tread of the tyres squealed across the thicker swathes of surface snow. The driver waved, and Maratse waved back, recognising the young, chubby face of Constable Aqqa Danielsen as he slowed the patrol car to a stop a few metres in front of Maratse and Seeri's team of dogs.

"Everything all right?" Maratse asked as

Danielsen climbed out of the patrol car. The wind plucked at the exhaust fumes as Danielsen left the engine running.

"Not really," Danielsen said. He waved at Seeri on his way over to Maratse. "They need you in Nuuk."

"Why?"

"Something about an old case." Danielsen shrugged. "They didn't say too much about it." He turned to point at Uummannaq Island in the distance. "They're sending a chopper. They sent me to pick you up."

"They want me to leave now?"

"*Aap.*"

Maratse looked down as the smallest of Seeri's dogs leaned into his leg. He reached down to tickle the dog's ears, then turned to look at Seeri. She pushed herself off the sledge and onto her feet. Danielsen stepped around Maratse to help her.

"Just imagine," Seeri said, eyes shining as Danielsen helped her walk across the ice to Maratse. "There I was, enjoying the company of a young man." She flashed a smile at Maratse and then curled a thin, wrinkled hand tightly around Danielsen's arm. "And then they send an even younger one to replace him."

"I'm sorry…" Maratse said.

Seeri brushed his apology away with a wave of her hand. "Don't be. You're needed in Nuuk."

"You heard what I said?" Danielsen asked.

"Young man," Seeri said. "I am neither deaf nor blind." She wagged a finger at Maratse as he started to laugh. "But I *do* need a little help once in a while.

I'm not too proud to admit it. But while the Constable is enjoying the big, bright lights of the city…"

"Aqqa will help with your dogs," Maratse said.

"I will?"

"*Iiji.*" Maratse caught the younger constable's eye and Danielsen nodded.

"I will," he said. "Of course, I will."

"And you'll take me back to town," Seeri said.

Danielsen looked at the patrol car. "They told me to fetch Maratse," he said.

"And now he is fetched." Seeri held onto Danielsen's arm as she reached for the fishing lure with the stubborn knot at the end of the line. "I'll make you a deal, *young* constable. If you can untie that knot…"

Maratse laughed as Seeri thrust the lure into Danielsen's hand. He crossed the ice to take Seeri's hand, wondering if he should offer to drive her back to town, only to remember the look on her face as the wind pinched her cheeks on the journey to the fishing hole. He didn't want to deprive her of the return journey, and as he caught her eye, he realised she would never have let him, anyway.

"Go," she said, with a nod at the patrol car. "Aqqa will take me home. They need you in Nuuk, Constable." Seeri squeezed Maratse's hand with a firmness that surprised him. "Be careful in the city," she said. "It wasn't built for the likes of you."

Maratse frowned as he thought about what she said, but Seeri simply pushed him away, smiling once, before turning to Aqqa to quiz him about his knowledge of dogs, and if she should be worried.

Maratse left them to it, waving once as he climbed into the patrol car, and once more as he turned the vehicle in a tight circle on the ice before straightening up for the drive back to Uummannaq.

He adjusted the rear-view mirror for a last look at Seeri, smiling as he saw her pointing at one dog, and then the next as Danielsen hooked them into their traces. Maratse knew Seeri's dogs would get her home even without Danielsen's help, but it pleased him to think she wouldn't be alone.

The patrol car bumped over the ridges of snow frozen into the troughs of the ice road. Maratse turned his attention to driving, letting his thoughts wander as he wondered which old case was important enough for Nuuk to send an unscheduled helicopter to pick him up. It would take him to the airport at Qaarsut, from where he imagined he would catch a regular flight, or perhaps even the King Air – the small, fast, twin-engine light aircraft operated by *Air Greenland* and reserved for emergencies.

As the heart-shaped mountain of Uummannaq drew closer, Maratse hoped it wasn't the King Air, for if it was, it could only mean one thing…

Trouble.

Part 3

Maratse caught the regular flight from Qaarsut, boarding *Air Greenland*'s bright red de Havilland Dash 7 shortly after the helicopter landed. The ground crew hurried him across the gravel strip and into the aircraft. A flight attendant settled Maratse in a seat at the rear of the Dash, turning a few passengers' heads as they got a look at the reason for the short delay. Delays due to weather or emergencies were the norm for Greenlanders and regular passengers, but waiting for a police constable was a little out of the ordinary, particularly so for the late-winter tourists. They threw a few last glances in Maratse's direction until the de Havilland's engines sputtered into life. All further thoughts of the curious late passenger were lost as the pilots coaxed the Arctic workhorse into life and thundered down the gravel strip before leaping into the air. Maratse closed his eyes, relieved he wasn't onboard the King Air, but curious all the same about why he had been summoned to Nuuk.

The constable who met Maratse at the airport knew little more than the time of the briefing, and that they were late.

"Sergeant Gaba will be furious," she said, leaning forward in her seat and gripping the wheel as she drove into town. She bobbed her head, clipping the oversized collar of her jacket with her tiny chin as drove.

"Sergeant Gaba?"

"*Aap*," the constable said, glancing at Maratse. "Sergeant *Alatak*. Sorry." The gears crunched as she pulled away from a sudden stop at the first roundabout. "He makes me nervous."

"Hmm."

The constable turned for a longer look at Maratse, frowning as she said, "What was that?"

"Nothing," Maratse said. He nodded at the car in front, and then slapped a hand on the dashboard when the constable braked hard.

"Sorry," she said, grinding the gears once more as the traffic started to move again.

"What's your name?" Maratse asked.

"Juulia Piaraq."

"From Nuuk?"

"From Ilulissat." Juulia smiled when Maratse frowned, as if he should know her. "I grew up I Denmark."

Maratse nodded, then again as Juulia talked him through a difficult childhood, changing schools, always being the odd one out, the Eskimo. Never *Inuit*. Never *Greenlander*. Just *different*.

"It was easier when I went to Gymnasium."

"In Denmark?"

"In Nuuk," Juulia said. "Down there." She smiled as she pointed down *H.J. Rinkip Aqqutaa* before turning left to drive the last few hundred metres to the police station. Juulia apologised when the patrol car shuddered, stalled, and stopped when she parked.

"You're nervous," Maratse said.

"It's Gaba…"

"Sergeant Gaba?" Maratse grasped the door handle, dipping his head in thanks as he got out of the car. "Don't worry about Gaba Alatak," he said. "Learn from him. Don't think about him."

"I'll try," Juulia said.

Maratse nodded one last time as Juulia took a moment to compose herself behind the wheel. He tapped the chest pocket of his jacket, contemplating a smoke before he entered the police station, and then stuffed his hands into his pockets. They sent a helicopter. Delayed a plane. He should probably go straight in. Maratse climbed the set of four steps into the police station and entered the long, low building. He wrinkled his nose in the heat, thought of Seeri and Danielsen on the ice, and smiled at the thought of Danielsen sorting Seeri's dogs once they got back to Uummannaq. He stopped at the door of the briefing room, nodded when a sergeant told him to go straight in, and then stepped inside.

The briefing room, like the station, was long, with folding chairs arranged in rows on two sides with an aisle in the middle. Maratse walked towards the low stage and podium at the far end, taking a seat in the second row to the left of the podium, when Gaba pointed at it.

Sergeant Gaba Alatak towered above Maratse even when he wasn't standing on the stage. He gripped the sides of the podium as he talked, glancing at the police commissioner, Lars Andersen, as he briefed the three police constables and one sergeant, none of whom Maratse recognised.

"And now we're all here," Gaba said, switching to English as he gestured at Maratse. "I think it's time we heard Mr Bennett's story. Sergeant Kuuitsi?"

Maratse turned his head as the sergeant pushed back his chair and stood up. He wore his black hair longer than Maratse, and next to Gaba's polished dome and statuesque physique, Sergeant Iaaku Kuuitsi looked positively scruffy. Maratse decided he liked him, if only for the fact they shared a common style of dress. The man Kuuitsi showed into the briefing room, however, was not someone Maratse had expected.

"Ah, hi," the man said, with an awkward wave at the police officers as Gaba gestured for him to join him on the stage. The man was tall, just a little shorter than Gaba, but much older. Maratse guessed he was in his mid-sixties. And American, judging by his accent.

"This is David Bennett," Gaba said, introducing him.

"You can call me *Dave*," the man said.

"All right." Gaba took a step back from the podium, making way for Dave as Sergeant Kuuitsi returned to his seat. "If you'll walk us through what happened, Dave."

"At the convention?"

"After that," Gaba said. He paused to look at Maratse, adding, "Dave attended the stamp collectors' convention at *Katuaq*." He waited for Maratse to nod, then continued, folding his muscular arms across his chest as he looked at

Maratse. "Akik Kamattoq – a local thug – was there. He followed Mr Bennett... Dave... back to his hotel."

"Ah, it was on the street, actually," Dave said. Gaba took another step back and gestured for the American to take over. "Ah, hi again," Dave said, looking at the police officers in front of him. He turned to Gaba. "Do we need a translator?"

"Please continue, Mr Bennett," the commissioner said.

"Right." Dave adjusted his glasses, ran a hand through his thick hair, then swallowed before speaking. "The man, Akik," he said, "took me back to my hotel. He knew where I was staying, and he came with me all the way to my room."

Maratse's chair creaked as he shifted in his seat. Gaba shot him a look, then encouraged Dave with a cough and a nod.

"When we got to my room, Akik said he wanted to see my cachets."

"Cachets?" the commissioner said.

Dave took a breath as he nodded. "Artwork on postcards."

"Just art?"

"For stamps, really," Dave said. "It's what I do. It's kind of a hobby."

"But you're a professional?"

"Artist? Yes." Dave's lips creased as he smiled. "I've done a lot of cachets for Greenland stamps. Some people like them."

"He's being modest, Commissioner," Kuuitsi said. "A lot of people like them."

"Including Akik," Gaba said. "And his

associates."

"Forgive me, Mr Bennett." The commissioner leaned back in his seat. "Please continue."

"About the cachets?"

The commissioner nodded.

"Well, Akik wanted to see them. I had some in my bag." Dave patted an imaginary satchel, then frowned as if he suddenly wondered where it was. He recovered a second later, apologising, before continuing. "I had more in the hotel room. In the safe. The small ones with the keypad." He mimed punching keys, then gave a nervous laugh as the police officers stared back at him. "Right. You know what a keypad is."

Gaba rescued Dave with another cough, and a glare at the constable sitting next to Kuuitsi, the one with the smirk on his face.

"Mr Bennett?" the commissioner said.

"Should I continue?"

"If you can." The commissioner glanced at Gaba, before adding, "We realise this was a traumatic experience."

"He certainly wasn't pleasant," Dave said.

Maratse frowned as he concentrated on the English words and Dave's American accent. His thoughts roamed as he wondered if Constable Petra Piitalaat Jensen was working, remembering she was good at English. Good at German. Perfect at Danish. Maratse smiled. Not so good at Greenlandic. He drifted a little more with a deeper frown on his forehead as he wondered why he would think about Petra. The soft crackle of Seeri's chuckle filtered through a mental blast of Arctic wind across the sea ice, distracting him further until a single name jerked Maratse out of his thoughts and back into the briefing room. Gaba glared at him as he leaned forward.

"Can you say that again?" Maratse said.

Dave turned to look at him. "Excuse me?"

"The name. What was it?"

"The girl's name?"

"*Iiji.*"

"Er…" Dave looked at Gaba for help.

"It's *Maratse* for *yes*," he said.

"Okay." Dave rested his hands on the podium. "Her name is Tiilla. Akik said she would be my contact. He wanted me to draw new cachets. I guess he saw me doing that at the convention. There was a lot of interest. But the cachets I have in the safe already have stamps on them. He didn't want them." Dave paused and then said. "He told me I should give the cachets to her, and only her."

"How old was she?" Maratse asked.

"Ah, he didn't say."

Maratse turned to Gaba.

"Eleven," Gaba said.

"From Uummannaq?"

Gaba dipped his bald head just once. "It's why you're here, Constable."

"Should I just…" Dave took a step back from the podium, relinquishing the stage to Maratse in anticipation of him taking over the briefing.

"Maratse's story can wait," Gaba said. "But now Constable Maratse is awake, I think you should finish your side of the story."

"There's not much more," Dave said, as he

resumed his place at the podium. "Akik said I should deliver my cachets to Tiilla." He paused for a second to look at Maratse, suddenly conscious that he had the constable's attention.

"And the purpose?" Gaba said, prompting Dave with a dip of his head.

"Of my cachets?" Dave shook his head. "He didn't say. But he only wanted the cachets with spaces for stamps. I think he wants to put stamps on them."

"We know he does," Kuuitsi said. "Commissioner?"

"Go ahead, Sergeant," the commissioner said.

Sergeant Kuuitsi joined Dave and Gaba on the stage. He made an effort to straighten his jacket, drawing more smirks from the officers in the front row. But it wasn't Gaba who reined in the younger constables. As soon as Kuuitsi started to speak, Maratse realised he did so with authority. While the men and women who knew Gaba respected him for his assertiveness in the field, it was Kuuitsi's years of experience on the streets of Nuuk and Copenhagen that made the men in the briefing room listen, Maratse included.

"As you know, Akik Kamattoq has been on my radar for a little while." Kuuitsi reached around Dave to pluck a remote from the podium. He aimed it at the projector suspended from the ceiling and clicked it. The screen behind the podium flickered into life and Kuuitsi used the remote to flick through a series of images of a man with a deep, angry scar on his chin. "Akik," he said, before flicking to the next image. "And more recently."

Dave fidgeted on the stage until Gaba nodded for him to take a seat. Maratse stared at the next image of a young girl, taller than he remembered, but with the same angular face and big brown eyes – sadder than he cared to think about.

"And Tiilla," Kuuitsi said, with a glance at Maratse. "We don't yet know how the girl is connected, what hold – if any – Akik has on her. But we're pretty sure we know why Akik is interested in Mr Bennett's artwork."

"And why is that?" the commissioner said.

"In a word? Drugs," Kuuitsi said. He flicked forward to the next image of an envelope with a stamp glued firmly to the top right-hand corner. "Samples, to be more precise."

"Samples of drugs?"

"*Aap.*" Kuuitsi held the remote by his side as he turned to address the commissioner. "It's an old trick, but new to Greenland. As you know, hash is our biggest problem."

"And long may it remain so," the commissioner said. "We don't want anything else."

"And neither do they," Kuuitsi said. He used the remote to flick through a series of photos of Greenlandic men aged between twenty and sixty. The constables nodded as they recognised the rogues' gallery of familiar drug dealers operating in Nuuk and the larger towns of Greenland. Kuuitsi stopped on an image of four men, then used the laser pointer on the remote to highlight Akik. "He thinks differently."

"Hard to believe," Gaba said.

"I know what you're thinking." Kuuitsi smiled

as if he and Gaba had had this discussion before. Many times. "There might be someone else behind Akik, pulling the strings. But until we know who, we have to assume it's just Akik. Working alone." Kuuitsi flicked the next image onto the screen. It was an older photo of a light aircraft on the ice, with the unmistakable twin peaks of Uummannaq mountain in the background. "Constable?" he said, turning to Maratse.

"*Iiji*," Maratse said. "I was there." He took a breath before adding, "And so was Tiilla."

Part 4

The distance from Maratse's seat to the podium was less than the width of a row of five chairs, but Maratse walked as if he was on the sea ice, sliding his feet over soft, thin patches, anticipating the moment when his toes dipped into the sea, and he should pull back quickly before the dark waters consumed him. The casual observer might think the constable was nervous, that he would rather not stand on the stage and address the room. Such an observation was not groundless. Maratse rarely spoke in front of a group, but in truth it was the thought of Tiilla lost and alone in Greenland's underworld, and how he, Maratse, might be responsible that gave him pause. And then he was at the podium, turning to the row of police officers Gaba had assembled for the operation, searching for the best way to start his part of the briefing.

"Tiilla Tinnaaq," he said, starting with the girl as he knew he would, "was nine years old when I met her. She and her half-brother Katu found a plane on the ice, a dead man in the pilot's seat, and a bag of money."

Gaba fidgeted as Maratse described the events on the ice in Uummannaq Fjord, how the girl – Tiilla – had found a pistol in the satchel, and the deal he had made with Katu to put things right.

"Tiilla is eleven now," Kuuitsi said, picking up

where Maratse left off. "A pretty girl, slowed down by a limp."

"She shot herself," Maratse said, adding, "She was lucky." His voice tailed off as he wondered just how lucky she had been, ending up in Nuuk, running with the likes of Akik and his associates.

Running.

Maratse's lips flattened into a grim smile as he imagined running was the last thing Tiilla could do.

"Is there anything more about the girl we should know, David?"

Maratse looked up as the commissioner spoke. He thought for a moment, then added what he knew, including the limited information he had about Tiilla's mother. "She had her demons," he said, and the men nodded.

"Demons?" Dave said, then quickly apologised, not wanting to interrupt.

"Alcohol," Gaba said. He nodded to Kuuitsi, mouthing *You're up* as he tugged Maratse's sleeve and pulled him to one side.

"The girl is the key," Kuuitsi said. "She's had a tough couple of years. Her mother succumbed to those demons, as did her half-brother. Katu committed suicide earlier this year. Tiilla bounced through a few families before they put her in the Children's Home in Nuuk. She ran away a few times, and we picked up each time. But this last time we lost track of her. Knowing what we do about Akik and his operation, it makes sense that he kept her out of sight, but purely for his own gains." Kuuitsi paused to whisper something in Greenlandic to Maratse, before continuing in English. "We're pretty sure Akik's interests do not include little girls. Whatever kind of man he might be, he lives by a certain, if not laudable, code. Plus, he has three sisters and a young daughter of his own in Sisimiut. We're not too concerned about Tiilla's wellbeing, but now we know where she is, we'll pull her out of there once the operation is over."

"You're going to use the girl as bait?"

"No, Mr Bennett," Gaba said, taking over. "We're using *you* as bait. We didn't know about the girl before you contacted us. But we flew Maratse down to Nuuk to give her a friendly..." Gaba glanced at Maratse, then corrected himself with a slight smirk on his lips. "A *familiar* face to earn her trust. But the truth is we don't know her location, and our best bet for getting her away from Akik is when she meets you to pick up the cachets."

"About those cachets." The commissioner took a moment, as if trying to figure out a particular detail before asking his question. He shook the thought out of his head, glanced at Dave and then directed his question to Kuuitsi. "Were talking about stamps and samples. Why not just stick a stamp on an envelope and send it wherever Akik plans to send it? Why not do that? He doesn't need Dave or his cachets."

Sergeant Kuuitsi nodded. The commissioner was known for asking the so-called *dumb questions*, just to make sure everyone was on the same page. He could have lightened the mood by adding, *I'm asking for a friend*, but that wasn't the commissioner's style. He wanted an open dialogue, and to create an atmosphere in which any question was valid, even if he already knew the answer.

Kuuitsi humoured him with a nod and a short answer, bringing everyone in the room up to speed.

"In a word, Commissioner – modernisation. New stamps come with a self-adhesive backing." Kuuitsi mimed peeling a stamp from a paper sheet. The old stamps had glue on the back, which reacted to saliva or a wet sponge. Akik needs old stamps."

"He can use old stamps," the commissioner said.

"He could, but they might draw attention."

"No more so than a fancy cachet drawn by Mr Bennett."

"True," Kuuitsi said. "But those fancy cachets attract a different kind of attention. My theory is Akik is playing smart. He wants collectibles. He's going to bring the stamps into Denmark as collector pieces."

"Which gives us the location of the meet in Copenhagen," Gaba said.

"A time and a place?" The commissioner stood up.

"A convention in the Bella Center. Just outside the city centre."

"I know where the Bella Center is, Sergeant," the commissioner said.

Gaba grinned, and said, "Just keeping you on your toes, sir."

"Well, now that I am on my *toes*." The commissioner made a show of pointing at his feet. "I have some calls to make." He looked at each member of Gaba's team, paused for a second as he studied Maratse's face, before settling his gaze on

Dave. "Mr Bennett?"

"Yes?"

"I think the plan is to tuck you away somewhere so you can draw your cachets."

"Yes, sir."

"But before you get started, I'm going to need a written statement from you. Plus, your signature on a document stating that you have freely and knowingly chosen to assist in this operation."

"I have," Dave said. "And I do."

"For which we are grateful, of course. But I'll need it in writing if I'm going to convince your embassy."

"There's an embassy in Nuuk?"

"Copenhagen," the commissioner said. "If you'll come with me, we'll let Gaba finish the briefing and see if we can't find your satchel."

"We're almost done," Gaba said. He waited for the commissioner to escort the American from the room before gesturing for the remaining police officers to form a casual circle on the stage. "SRU is not deploying on this one," he said in Greenlandic. "But as leader of the Special Response Unit, I will be taking point. All tactical decisions will be made by me, while Sergeant Kuuitsi has command of the operation. Iaaku?"

Kuuitsi nodded. "I know Akik, his operation, and his contacts. This little stunt of his is designed to get the attention of the big boys in Copenhagen. There are two things at play here." Kuuitsi held out his hand and straightened his index finger. "One. We need to know how he got hold of the drugs to mix his sample. Personally, I doubt he cooked it up himself, so we need to know who he's working with. It could be a temporary hospital worker or a lab technician with access to the good stuff. Either way, we need evidence before Akik gets a chance to destroy it."

"Plain clothes, gentlemen," Gaba said, nodding for Kuuitsi to continue.

"Then there's the American. We need to ensure his safety, obviously. We can't have a dead American on Greenland soil. It just doesn't look good." Kuuitsi waited as the men laughed, then glanced at Maratse, who gave him a tight-lipped stare. "Mr Bennett delivers the artwork to the girl. We follow the girl to Akik. It's that simple."

"And Tiilla?" Maratse said. "What about her?"

"That's why you're here, Constable," Gaba said. "She knows you."

"We've met," Maratse said. "She doesn't *know* me."

"Maybe not, but she knows what you're capable of. She'll trust you." Gaba excused himself and pulled Maratse to one side, lowering his voice as he added, "I read the report. It was interesting. Especially the part about the plane exploding."

"That's what happened." Maratse held Gaba's gaze.

"Sure," Gaba said, dipping his head and breaking eye contact, if only for a second. When he looked at Maratse again, he was all business, prodding him in the chest with a knuckle as he spoke. "But we both know you left out the part about *how* the plane exploded." Gaba let his hand drop and gestured at Maratse's pistol. "We're missing a ballistics report. Not to mention the plane."

"It sank," Maratse said. "After the explosion."

"Convenient."

Maratse shrugged. "It's Greenland. The ice broke. The plane sank."

"And two very bad men disappeared along with it." Gaba let out a soft laugh. "You know, Constable, there are times when you frustrate me, and other times when I can't help but admire your audacity."

"Hmm."

"And that, there," Gaba said, prodding Maratse's chest for a second time. "That whole non-committal crap you pull. It works. Annoyingly. And nobody asks questions. They just let it go. That's a fine trick you've got there, Constable. And while it might work further north, you're in the city now. Remember that."

"Gaba," Maratse said, when the SRU leader had finished his lecture.

"What?"

"That report."

"*Aap*. What about it?"

"Did you read the part about me acting alone, because I was the only officer on duty?"

"It was mentioned."

"And that SRU did not respond."

"*Couldn't* respond, Constable," Gaba said. "There's a difference."

"*Iiji*," Maratse said, with a nod of his head.

Gaba's nostrils flared as he took a long breath. "Careful, Constable," he said. "This isn't the time to piss me off."

"I'm not trying to."

"You're not?"

"*Eeqqi*." Maratse shook his head. He pointed at the men gathered around Kuuitsi. "There are no women on the team." He waited for Gaba to respond, and then added, "We need one. For Tiilla."

"Fine," Gaba said. "Only your usual squeeze – Petra – is not here."

"*Squeeze?*"

Gaba sighed, and said, "Never mind. I'll assign you a female officer for the duration of the operation."

"What about Juulia Piaraq?" Maratse asked.

Gaba took a moment, then smiled. "Sure. She's all yours."

"*Qujanaq.*"

"Don't thank me yet. It's a bit premature, Constable. Besides," Gaba said, "you and Piaraq are babysitting the American. He needs to draw. The two of you can stay with him until he's done."

"And Tiilla?"

"We'll come to that."

Gaba turned away to join Kuuitsi and the other officers. Maratse slipped out of the briefing room and headed for the main door. He found a spot in the parking area, brushed at the more stubborn slush and old patches of old snow on the ground with his boot, and then lit a cigarette. He rolled the cigarette into the gap between his teeth on the right side of his mouth and stuffed his hands into his pockets. Maratse closed his eyes, picturing Tiilla a few years younger, and the pain that lanced through her face each time she moved her foot. It would get better; the nurse had promised him. It would heal. Only some things never healed.

Maratse smoked, lost in his thoughts, until a cough disturbed him, and he opened his eyes as the American walked towards him.

"May I join you?" Dave asked.

Maratse nodded, then plucked the packet of cigarettes from his pocket, offering them to Dave.

"Ah, I don't smoke," he said. Dave smiled as Maratse slipped the cigarette packet back into his pocket. "But if I'm not bothering you, I wonder if I could ask you something?"

"*Iiji*," Maratse said.

Dave frowned, dipping his head as if he might catch the word again.

"It means *yes*," Maratse said. "In East Greenland."

"You're not from Nuuk?"

Maratse shook his head. "Ittoqqortoormiit," he said.

"On the east coast?"

"*Iiji.*"

"But you know the girl." Dave pointed at the police station. "From the slide?"

"Tiilla," Maratse said. "We met in Uummannaq." He finished his cigarette, then added, "I move around a lot."

"Never in one place, eh?" Dave shuffled his feet as if he too, suffered from a certain restlessness. "I was in the army. In my youth. I drove tanks." Dave paused, only to continue when Maratse gave him an encouraging nod of the head. "I didn't *see* as

40

much of the world as I might have liked, but I saw a lot of birds."

"Birds?"

"Wildlife," Dave said. "My other passion, other than stamps."

"I like birds," Maratse said.

"I thought so." Dave gestured, adjusted his satchel, then looked at Maratse's sunburned face. He smiled as he plucked a fish scale from the sleeve of Maratse's jacket. "You're not like the others," he said. "You're closer to nature, somehow."

"Everyone is close to nature in Greenland," Maratse said.

"I'm sure that's true, Constable. Only, you seem *closer*. If you know what I mean?"

It wasn't something Maratse thought about. Nature was just a part of his life, his identity. But if he *did* think about it, he would have to agree. He was closer to nature than Gaba with his smartly fitting uniform, and the care he took in his appearance. Gaba belonged in the city. He fared well in almost all environments. Maratse, however, was at his best on the ice.

"Gaba is a good officer," Maratse said.

"I'm sorry? What?"

"You were talking about the others."

"Actually, Constable, I was talking about you."

"My mistake," Maratse said. "My English…"

"Is perfectly adequate," Dave said. "But now that you mention it, I am a little nervous." Dave paused as a patrol car bumped into the parking area and shuddered to a stop beside them. The driver waved at Maratse, then jabbed her finger at the passenger side for Maratse to get in.

"Come on," Maratse said, opening the rear passenger door for Dave to get climb in the back.

"Ah, and who is this?"

"Constable Piaraq," Maratse said as Juulia wound the window down to shake Dave's hand.

"And where are we going?"

"Coffee and a pep talk," Juulia said with a barely suppressed giggle. She smiled at Maratse, eyes shining, as she switched to Greenlandic, chattering her way through a long explanation about how excited she was to be on the team, and how grateful she was Maratse had put in a good word for her with Gaba.

"You're welcome," Maratse said, continuing in English.

"Oh, right," Juulia said. "English, for him."

"For me," Dave said as he buckled his seatbelt. "Much appreciated. But I'm supposed to stay here and draw the new cachets."

"You need inspiration," Maratse said.

"I suppose so," Dave said. He removed his glasses, cleaned them, and then studied Maratse as if something else was going on.

"And you have everything you need?"

Dave patted the satchel beside him. "I do."

"Okay then." Juulia gripped the wheel. "Which café?"

"A busy one," Maratse said.

Juulia bumped the car into gear and then took off, braking at the exit of the parking area.

"Seatbelts might be a good idea," she said with an apologetic shrug of her shoulders.

"Hmm," Maratse said.

Part 5

Maratse pressed a handful of Danish kroner into Juulia's hands and then found a table in the large bay window looking out onto the semi-pedestrianised street, *Imaneq*. When Dave queried the exposed nature of the table, Maratse grunted something about *good light*.

"That's true, of course," Dave said as Maratse pulled back a chair and encouraged him to sit facing the window. "Do you know much about art, Constable?"

Maratse shrugged, then pulled out a chair beside Dave. He arranged it in front of the window, looking out, and said, "I know about light."

"Really?"

"*Iiji*," Maratse said, with a nod. "The ice reflects the light. In winter, when the moon is shining, the light is reflected up to the sky. Not much, but enough to see by. On a clear night with a full moon, it's just as bright as daylight, only concentrated." Maratse frowned as he struggled to find more English words to describe it. When Juulia returned with three large lattes, Maratse used her to describe what he was trying to say. Dave looked from one constable to the other as they traded Greenlandic words across the table.

"It's not *daylight*," Juulia said, warming her hands around the mug of coffee as she waited for

Maratse to explain. "But brighter than a winter with no ice. There are still shadows, of course, but they are thinner – you can see through them. But the shadows in the summer are stronger…"

"Because the light is stronger," Dave said, nodding.

"And *longer*," Maratse said. He peered at the coffee, frowned, then took a sip.

Dave watched him.

"You're quite the enigma, Constable," he said, as Maratse looked up. "You think about light, and all its facets, and yet you don't know what to make of Italian coffee."

"I don't like milk," Maratse said.

"But you chose this café," Juulia said. "If you don't like it, you should have said."

"I like it." Maratse took another sip of coffee, then a gulp, wiping his mouth with the back of his hand. "I like the coffee."

"But you don't," Juulia said.

"Hmm."

"Ah, and there it is, Constable. I've been waiting for your next *humph*."

Maratse turned to the American, and Dave shrank a little under his scrutiny. "Forgive me," he said. "That was too familiar. Only, I feel like I have known you a long time, and no time at all. Which makes no sense – none at all." Dave reached for his coffee, took a sip, and reset. "What I mean," he said, placing the mug back on the table. "What I'm trying to say…"

Juulia lifted her mug to her lips, hiding her smile behind the mug as she peered over the lip at

Maratse, then Dave, wondering if she should intervene. Maratse broke the tension with a single word.

"Draw."

"*Draw?*" Dave glanced at the pistol holstered above Maratse's hip and swallowed. "I'm not sure."

Maratse reached for the satchel Dave had slung over the back of the chair.

"Right," Dave said, as he took the hint. "*Draw* not draw," he said.

Maratse stared at him, then nodded as Dave took out a sketch pad of cartridge paper.

Juulia leaned to one side and whispered in Dave's left ear. "I'm not sure the Constable is into Westerns," she said.

Dave nodded. "I'm not sure he is."

"Hmm," Maratse said. He pushed his coffee to one side and then stood up. He stared out of the window for a moment, then turned towards the counter. Juulia gave him the change from the first round of coffee, and he left them to it.

"He can be a little touchy, I guess," Juulia said once Maratse reached the counter.

Dave took out a tin of pencils and arranged them on the table. "You know him well, I suppose?"

"Not at all." Juulia smiled, adding, "We met this afternoon. Gaba ordered me to pick him up. I tried to say I wouldn't recognise him, which is when Gaba – Sergeant Alatak," she said, straightening her back. "The *Sergeant* said I should look out for *a hunter pretending to be a policeman.*"

"*Pretending?*"

"Exactly," Juulia said. "That's exactly what I thought. And then I said I supposed it would be easy enough to spot him as he would be in uniform."

Dave reached into his satchel to find an errant eraser that had escaped the tin, and then paused, smiling at the word uniform.

"*Aap*," Juulia said, eyes glistening as she recalled the next part of the conversation. "And do you know what Gab... *Sergeant* Alatak said?"

"I could guess," Dave said, "but no. Not really."

"He said *barely*." Juulia giggled. "About the uniform." Her giggle turned into a laugh, loud enough that she hiccupped and pressed her hand over her mouth. Juulia recovered and took a sip of coffee before adding, "Honestly, I got a bit mixed up. I mean, would he barely be in uniform, which might mean he was naked. Or were his clothes barely fit to be called a uniform?"

Dave glanced over his shoulder as Maratse returned to the table. He leaned in close to Juulia for a conspiratorial whisper, and said, "The latter. Definitely."

Maratse slid a large cup of thick black coffee onto the table and sat down. "Espresso," he said, as Juulia leaned over the table for a closer look. "Four espressos."

"All right then," Juulia said. She leaned back in her chair and watched as Dave started to draw.

"Juulia," Maratse said.

"What?"

"I need you to look out of the window."

"I'm watching him draw."

"That can wait."

Juulia took a last look at Dave's sketch pad, squinting as she tried to guess what he was drawing, and then moved her chair into a better position with a good view of the street outside the window.

"I thought we were supposed to have our back to the wall and keep an eye on the door," she said, tapping her mug with her nails.

"Only in Westerns," Maratse said. Juulia's face flushed as he caught her eye.

"You heard," she said.

Maratse shrugged. "I like science fiction."

"Really?" Dave put his pencil down. "You like sci-fi? I would never have guessed. Who is your favourite author?"

Maratse didn't answer. Dave reached forward to tap his arm, as if Maratse hadn't heard him, but then pulled back as Maratse pushed away from the table.

"Stay with him, Juulia," Maratse said, and bolted out of the café.

Maratse heard little more than a shout and the slamming of the café door as he pounded onto the street, bumping past a small group of three teenagers, stumbling around an older man and his walker – Maratse stopped long enough to steady the man on his feet and apologise – before darting through the crowd of shoppers as they parted to both sides. A small figure wearing black jeans, big black boots, and a dark grey hoodie ran ahead of Maratse. Youth was on her side, but a limp in her right leg slowed her down.

Tiilla Tinnaaq gritted her teeth and ran. She

bounced off an older man, splitting the plastic bag he carried as it caught on her boot buckle, and spilling the contents onto the street. The man yelled at her, lunged for her shoulder, and caught the tip of Tiilla's hood in his fist. He yanked Tiilla onto the ground and dragged her back to his shopping, pointing at the different items, shouting at her to pick them up, only to let go of Tiilla as Maratse barrelled into him. The man fell to the ground with Maratse sprawled on top of him. Tiilla picked herself up, glanced once at Maratse, frowned as she saw his face, and then ran.

"Tiilla! Stop!"

Maratse pushed off the man and ran, kicking a tin further along the street and drawing another shout from the man as he cursed Maratse, cursed the police, and most of all, the girl.

"You'd better lock her up," the man shouted after Maratse. "It's the last thing you'll do before you get fired. You'll see."

Maratse ignored him.

Tiilla twisted into a narrow gap between two shops, dragging her right leg as she tried to keep going, to run faster, only to slow down each time she looked over her shoulder at Maratse.

He closed the gap.

Tiilla grabbed a loose bag of rubbish in the alleyway and hurled it at him. Maratse batted it to one side. She found a bottle, grabbed it, turned, and threw it at Maratse's chest. The bottle bounced off Maratse and smashed on the ground. The shards of glass grated under his feet as he kept going.

"Tiilla," he said, slowing to catch his breath.

"Tiilla, stop."

Tiilla reached the end of the alleyway, pressed her fists on a large dumpster blocking her way, and pounded the sides, screaming once before she turned to glare at Maratse. She stuffed her right hand into the front pocket of her hoodie and pulled out an old fishing knife. The blade was pocked with rust, the plastic handle scratched and bleached in the sun, but it fit well in the palm of her hand, giving Maratse pause, just as Tiilla intended.

The chase ended there, at the end of the alleyway, with a police constable, a young girl, and a knife.

"Tiilla," Maratse said. "You know me."

"I don't know anyone," she spat.

Maratse swallowed as he stared at the young girl's face, the bruise on her left cheek, her bottom lip – split, scabbed, and bloody. He looked at her eyes, searching for the soft brown eyes he remembered when sitting by her bed in the hospital in Uummannaq. She was wounded then, haunted now. What was left of her childhood when he saw her last had been stripped away. Maratse let his hands fall to his sides and nodded.

"Tiilla," he said. "You knew me, once."

"I never."

"*Iiji*," he said. "You did. And I knew you and your brother."

"Half-brother," Tiilla said.

"Katu."

"*Naamik*." New blood burst from the cut on Tiilla's lip as she looked at Maratse and sneered. "Katu's dead," she said. "They're all dead."

"*Eeqqi*," Maratse said. He took a small step towards her. "Not everyone. You are still alive, Tiilla. Let me help you."

Tiilla twisted the knife in her hand as Maratse took another step towards her. He stopped. Tiilla grinned, then lifted the knife to press the tip of the rusted blade into her throat.

"Tiilla," Maratse whispered. "Don't."

"You think you can help me?"

Maratse nodded. "I want to."

"You can't. Because I don't belong to you, *Constable*." Another sneer, more blood on her lip, and a red mark on her skin where she pressed the knife harder.

"You don't belong to anyone," Maratse said.

"Then you don't know anything. Do you?"

"I know you, Tiilla." Maratse took a breath, another step. "I know I can help you."

Tiilla leaned to the left to look around Maratse as a man walked into the alleyway. Maratse saw Tiilla's eyes widen at the man's approach. He wondered for a second, how such young eyes could look so old, so sad, and then he knew who Tiilla belonged to, and guessed that when he turned around, he would see the man from Kuuitsi's slide, the man with the deep scar scored into his chin.

Only it wasn't.

Maratse whirled away from the man to look at Tiilla, just as she clambered up the side of the dumpster, dropping her knife as she reached the top. Tiilla swore, turning for her knife, just as Maratse picked it up. She looked into his eyes, squinting at him in the shadow of the alley, giving Maratse a split second of hope, before she spun around, slipped onto her bottom, and slid over the other side of the dumpster.

"Tiilla! Wait!"

Maratse sighed at the sound of Tiilla running away. He tucked her knife into his belt and then turned to face the man whose shopping he had spilled on the streets of Nuuk.

"I hope she was worth it, Constable," the man said. "I have powerful friends."

"Hmm," Maratse said, as he reached for his cigarettes.

Part 6

A swirl of blue light splashed on the walls of the alleyway and the man turned just as Juulia opened the driver's door and hopped out of the patrol car. Maratse watched as she guided the man to one side with a gentle touch of his elbow, a sympathetic nod, and a string of reassuring words that seemed to put the man at ease. The bag of shopping Juulia retrieved from the passenger seat was the final touch, and she sent the man on his way with little more than a sneer than aimed at Maratse as he walked back onto the street. Juulia slipped her hands into her trouser pockets and dipped her head to one side. The smile on her lips suggested she had done well, had smoothed the edges of an otherwise unpleasant encounter, and was now ready to receive a word or two of appreciation from Maratse.

"Hmm," he said, as he finished his cigarette.

"That's it?" Juulia dipped her head towards Maratse, expecting more but with an air of one who should perhaps settle for less.

"Tiilla's gone," he said.

"I know."

"I tried to talk to her."

"I noticed." Juulia pointed at the patrol car. "We followed…"

"The American?"

"Is back at the station. Gaba called. He said

there's been a development. He said you should come back."

Maratse turned to look at the dumpster, shifting his feet as if contemplating climbing over it. But the trail was cold.

"And Gaba's waiting," Juulia said.

Maratse took a last look in the direction Tiilla had run and then followed Juulia back to the car. She gestured at the driving seat, and Maratse shook his head.

"You drive."

"You're sure?"

"*Iiji*," Maratse said as he climbed into the passenger seat.

Juulia settled behind the wheel, took a breath, and slowly shifted into first gear. She eased her foot off the clutch and giggled as the heavy patrol car rolled forward.

"Like butter on warm bread," Juulia said. She glanced at Maratse, then accelerated. "You're the only one – the only *man* who hasn't commented on my driving."

Maratse turned to her and said, "You can drive."

"*Aap*. But…"

"You'll get better."

"I know, but everyone else makes such a big deal out of it. When I was at the academy, I aced all the theory, even the physical stuff. But they failed my driving." Juulia shrugged, and said, "I've been given a dispensation. Provided I get better…"

"Hmm," Maratse said. He nodded at the road as Juulia pulled off the pedestrianised street and turned the patrol car in the direction of the station. "You're better than when we met earlier," he said.

"*Qujanaq.*"

Juulia drove the last few hundred metres in silence, leaving Maratse to his thoughts. But when she parked, and Maratse reached for the door handle, Juulia stopped him with a light touch on his arm.

"The girl's important to you. Isn't she?"

"I failed her," Maratse said.

"I don't think so. You're not responsible for what happened."

"*Imaqa.*" Maratse slid his hand around the door handle. He opened it a crack, and then paused. "I won't fail her again," he said, and stepped out of the car.

Gaba snapped his fingers at Maratse as soon as they entered the police station. The smooth walls of the narrow corridor outside the briefing room buzzed with conversation drifting from pockets of police officers going over last details. Juulia caught her breath as she followed Maratse and Gaba into the briefing room.

"I've never seen so many officers. It's like you called in the whole department," she said.

"I did." Gaba snapped his fingers again and pointed at two empty chairs in the front row in front of the low stage. The podium had been moved to one side and Dave was busy laying out his cachets on top of it. Sergeant Kuuitsi stood beside him, counting and nodding as Dave placed one card on top of the next. "Here's what's new," Gaba said, once Maratse and Juulia were seated.

Gaba's briefing, like Gaba himself, was pared to the bone and punctuated with jabs of his fingers as he allocated Maratse to Kuuitsi's detail, together with Juulia.

"You'll do exactly what the sergeant says," Gaba said. He glanced at Juulia, but let his gaze linger on Maratse as he waited for him to confirm he understood. "Constable?" he said, when Maratse took too long to answer.

"I do what Kuuitsi says."

"That's right. He has command of the operation, and I need to know you understand your role."

"We stay with Sergeant Kuuitsi," Juulia said. "We understand."

"Of course you do," Gaba said. "But the stakes are higher now. "Somehow, Akik managed to convince his contacts to come to Nuuk. The big boys are on their way. They should arrive tomorrow, by boat."

"They sailed from Denmark?" Juulia asked.

"They flew to Narsarsuaq a few days ago. They're sailing up the coast."

"Then they don't need the cachets," Juulia said.

Maratse turned to look at Gaba. "They still need them. Akik is showing off."

"Which is typical for Akik," Gaba said. "He's never been the smartest tool in the box. But he's eager. Can't fault him for that. He thinks he's on to something big, and that he has the answer to slipping drugs in and out of the country."

"On the backs of old stamps glued to fancy cachets," Juulia said. "It seems too easy, and stupid."

"It is," Gaba said. He turned as a younger sergeant called from the briefing room door. "Stay here," he said to Maratse. "I'll be back."

Juulia waited until Gaba was gone, then whispered to Maratse, "I might be on probation, but this seems too easy. Akik must know we're working with the American. If he didn't before, then if Tiilla saw us in the café…"

"She did," Maratse said.

Juulia's lips spread in a slow smile as she caught on. "You wanted her to see us."

"*Iiji.*"

"You don't care about the operation."

Maratse turned to Juulia and dipped his head ever so slightly.

"You only care about Tiilla."

"I care about lots of things, but right now…" Maratse nodded again. "Only Tiilla."

"Then what's *really* going on?" Juulia tapped her thigh, then lifted her finger to point at Kuuitsi. "The sergeant said he's been observing Akik and his associates for some time."

"*Iiji.*"

"They wanted to follow the drugs all the way to Denmark, to find out who Akik is selling to."

"They did."

"But something's not right. Is it?" Juulia frowned, and then said, "We can't make drugs like this in Greenland."

"We could," Maratse said. "We don't."

"So Akik isn't selling. He's…"

"Negotiating," Maratse said, a split second

before Juulia.

"And Kuuitsi knows? He must do."

"The sergeant knows," Maratse said. "I think he knows a lot."

"And Gaba?"

Maratse nodded.

The door to the briefing room opened. Kuuitsi looked up from the podium and waved as the commissioner entered. He glanced at Maratse, nodded once, then turned back to examine the cachets. The commissioner beckoned to Maratse and nodded for him to follow him.

"Stay with the American," Maratse said to Juulia as he stood up.

"What about you?"

Maratse shrugged. "I don't know. But I'll find you later."

The commissioner shook Maratse's hand as he joined him, greeting him as if he had just arrived. "There wasn't time to welcome you properly earlier," he said, adding, "I hope we didn't drag you away from anything important, Constable."

"Nothing Aqqa can't handle," Maratse said, thinking of Constable Danielsen sledging back to Uummannaq with Seeri and her dogs.

"Of course," the commissioner said. "I know Aqqa." He paused as they entered the corridor, then pointed to the wide metal and wood staircase leading to the first floor. "I thought we could have a little chat in my office," he said.

The commissioner led the way, taking the stairs with long strides, two at a time. Maratse hurried to follow him. At the top of the stairs, the commissioner turned left, leading Maratse into an open office with several desks arranged in rows, before stopping at the door of his office and gesturing for Maratse to go inside. The blinds hanging on the office windows were drawn.

"I'll grab some coffee," the commissioner said. "I'll just be a minute."

Maratse reached for the handle, then stopped as the door opened from the inside.

"Come in, Constable," Gaba said.

"Hmm," Maratse said.

Gaba took Maratse's arm and pulled him into the office. He shut the door, then waited for Maratse to sit on the couch pressed against the long interior wall. Gaba walked to the commissioner's desk and leaned against it, saying nothing, until the commissioner returned with a thermos jug of coffee and three large mugs.

"So, Constable," the commissioner said, once he had poured the coffee. "There's a reason you're here."

"Besides Tiilla," Gaba said. He took a mug from the low table in front of the couch, and then leaned against the wall, staring at Maratse between flicking his gaze at the door, as if expecting someone to come rushing in at any moment.

The commissioner sat down at the opposite end of the couch. Air leaked out of the leather cushions as he settled into a comfortable position. Maratse took a sip of coffee and waited.

"Two years ago," the commissioner said. "You intercepted a light aircraft on the sea ice on Uummannaq Fjord."

"It was an emergency landing," Maratse said. "The pilot was sick. He landed..."

"And died," the commissioner said. He ran his hand through closely cropped and slightly greying hair. "I read the report. And I know about the gun, Tiilla's injury, and the money, of course. But we also know the pilot was testing a route to see if it was viable to cross Greenland and run drugs from Canada to Svalbard, or the other way around. It doesn't matter, really. What matters, is this..." The commissioner nodded at Gaba to continue, and then leaned back in the couch.

"You were alone in Uummannaq," Gaba said.

"*Iiji,*" Maratse said and nodded. "Training courses..."

"And leave," Gaba said. "An unfortunate coincidence."

"Unless it was planned," the commissioner said. He looked at Gaba and grinned. "Sorry, Sergeant. I stole your punch line."

"*Aap,*" Gaba said. "I forgive you, sir. But," he said, turning back to Maratse. "I can't forgive or ignore the fact that whoever gave permission for leave and training to occur at the same time may have had ulterior motives."

"Constable," the commissioner said. "What Sergeant Alatak is saying is that we think someone planned for you to be alone, knowing that the chosen route would take the pilot over Uummannaq. There are precious few police officers dotted around Greenland as it is, but leaving a skeleton staff of just one man in Uummannaq was no coincidence."

Gaba pushed off the wall to stand, and said, "If

the plane needed to land in an emergency…"

"It did," Maratse said.

"*Aap.* But I don't think anyone could imagine the pilot would have a heart attack. But it was anticipated that in the event of an emergency, one constable alone in Uummannaq would pose very little threat to the operation."

"But they got that wrong," the commissioner said. "Didn't they, David?"

"*Iiji*," Maratse said.

"And we're hoping they're going to get it wrong again," Gaba said.

Maratse's brow creased as he put the pieces together.

"The big players," he said. "They're not Danish."

"They're not," the commissioner said.

"And Tiilla…" Maratse rested his mug on his thigh. "She's not the go between."

"She's not, Constable." The commissioner shifted position and then turned to look at Maratse. "She's bait."

"Bait?" Maratse paused again, struggling once more with the pieces of a puzzle that seemed to get more complicated by the second. He took a breath, then shook his head as the plot escaped him.

"Akik isn't selling drugs, David," the commissioner said. "He's selling you."

"Me?"

"The players are American, David." The commissioner gestured for Gaba to continue.

"They tried to recover the money from the plane that landed on the ice." Gaba nodded as the pieces of Maratse's puzzle started to fit together. "You stopped them, Constable. You cost them money and time. But they never forgot."

"And Akik?"

"Used Tiilla to get to you." Gaba snorted, and said, "But before you start thinking Akik is smarter than he looks, you need to take one step further."

"He had help," Maratse said.

"*Aap.*" Gaba grinned as Maratse took a slow sip of coffee. "Now you're getting it," he said.

Maratse swallowed the last of his coffee, then slid the mug onto the table. He tapped his thigh, then looked from Gaba to the commissioner. "But what about the American?" he asked. "Is he one of them?"

"That," the commissioner said, as he stood up. "Is a very good question."

Part 7

Gaba caught up with Maratse on the stairs, clapping a large hand on the constable's shoulder, jerking him to a sudden stop as if he had dug an anchor into the ice to arrest a determined team of dogs. Maratse bristled at the end of an imaginary gangline, shrugging the sergeant's hand from his shoulder as he turned to look at him.

"You can't do that, Constable," Gaba said, letting his hand fall to his side. "You can't just burst out of the commissioner's office like that."

"Like what?" Maratse clenched his fists by his sides, tapped his thighs with the scarred and chapped skin typical of a hunter's knuckles.

"Half-cocked," Gaba said. "With a half-baked plan in your head."

"I don't have a plan," Maratse said, drawing a grim smile across Gaba's lips.

"Of course you don't. Why would I ever think you did?"

Maratse turned for the stairs. Gaba stopped him again, gentler the second time.

"It's not you against the world, Constable. Or you against the Americans." He paused, let his hand fall again, then jabbed a thick finger at Maratse's chest. "You have to learn to trust other people, Constable."

"I trust people."

Gaba snorted. "Sure. I know you do. But that's not what I said." The big SRU sergeant lowered his voice as two constables squeezed past them on their way down the stairs. "I said *other* people. Specifically," he said, sighing. "You have to trust me." Gaba looked at Maratse's fists, then nodded as Maratse unclenched them. "I've taken steps," Gaba said, lowering his deep voice to a rumbling whisper. He leaned in closer to Maratse. "This is a closed group. We keep it tight. The focus is on the American, the stamps. We keep everyone focused on that and leave the other thing between us."

"Who?" Maratse asked.

"You, me, Kuuitsi, and the commissioner."

"Kuuitsi?"

"*Aap*," Gaba said, pulling back, and raising his voice to a normal, if slightly subdued level. "He knows the case, the history, and he knows Akik."

"And we can trust him?"

"You can trust *me*, Constable," Gaba said. "I've taken steps."

Maratse held Gaba's gaze for a second. "Hmm," he said, and started down the stairs. Gaba called after him, but Maratse kept going. He turned for the briefing room at the bottom of the stairs, then caught a wave from Juulia standing outside the door of the guest toilet. He adjusted course and stomped across the hall towards her.

"He's inside," Juulia said.

Maratse grunted, took Juulia's arm in a gentle but insistent grip, and then slapped his hand on the door. He pulled Juulia inside before she could protest, nodding for her to stand to one side as he turned and locked the door.

"Constable?" Dave said, as he stepped out of a cubicle. "What's going on?"

Maratse said nothing. He gestured at the sink and waited for Dave to wash his hands.

"Drugs," Maratse said, once Dave was finished.

"Yes?"

"I don't care about them."

Dave glanced at Juulia, frowning as she shrugged her shoulders. "Ah," he said. "I suppose I know what that means, or perhaps I'm *supposed* to."

"Maratse," Juulia said as he took a step towards Dave, forcing the American to back up against the counter. "Maratse, stop."

"I don't care about drugs," Maratse repeated. The toes of Maratse's boots bumped against the American's as he stared into his face. "I only care about…"

"The girl," Juulia said. She placed her hand on Maratse's shoulder, pulling him back a few centimetres, then a couple more. "You care about Tiilla."

"*Iiji*," Maratse said. He kept his eyes on Dave.

"I think we all do." Juulia pushed Maratse back a little further, giving Dave room to breathe, to think, to recover. "Dave is just trying to help. He *can* help," she said, encouraging the American with a nod of her head.

"I want to," Dave said, adding, "Even if I don't really know what's going on."

"Hmm," Maratse said.

"Ah," Dave said, smiling as the tension eased.

"But *that* I do know. I think I'm catching on, Constable. If I may?" Maratse frowned as Dave reached out to shake his hand. "I don't know Greenlandic. Can't speak a word of Danish and admit to being thoroughly humbled by the command of English you..." he glanced at Juulia. "... and your fellow officers have demonstrated since I arrived. But grunting," he said, grinning as he gripped Maratse's hand. "*That* I understand." Dave let go of Maratse, straightened his back, and said, "If I may be so bold, I surmise you are in a bind, Constable."

"A bind?"

"Ah, yes," Dave said, pausing as he searched for another word. "You have a problem, but," he said, wagging a finger before anyone interrupted him. "It's not the obvious one. Is it?"

"*Eeqqi*," Maratse said.

Dave turned to Juulia. She smiled, and said, "*Maratse* for *no*."

"Thank you," Dave said. He turned back to Maratse. "This is more complicated than my stamps and the young girl."

Maratse nodded.

"And," Dave said, pressing his hands together as he warmed to the subject. "The *bind* you are in means you have some doubts about the people around you." Dave raised his hand, nodding, as he said, "I apologise. I've read far too many crime books and seen way too many TV shows not to recognise the classic restroom scene."

It was Maratse's turn to look at Juulia for help.

"When they meet in the shuttle on a starship,"

she said, translating the crime scene into Maratse's more familiar science fiction genre. "Oh," she said, as Maratse frowned at her. "You just wanted the word for *restroom*." Juulia's cheeks coloured as she gestured at the cubicle doors. "Toilets," she said, and Maratse nodded.

"A quiet place to talk," Dave said. "In private."

Maratse tucked his hands into his jacket pockets, took a breath, and said, "I need your help."

Sergeant Iaaku Kuuitsi leaned over the podium, nodding as the commissioner exchanged a few words, before clearing his throat to call the police officers assembled in the briefing room to order. It was a larger group than he had addressed earlier, and the heightened tension was palpable, not least because of the presence of Sergeant Gaba Alatak and the three additional members of the SRU standing in a line by the door. Kuuitsi coughed again, waited for the men and women to settle, and then began.

"Akik Kamattoq," he said, clicking the remote to project Akik's image onto the screen, "has some interesting friends. Kuuitsi clicked the remote again, and the image changed to a grainy shot of two men walking through the tiny airport lounge of Narsarsuaq Airport in the south of Greenland. The men's features were obscured, but their skin tone was clearly white. "I have to admit," Kuuitsi said, turning back to the assembled officers, "Akik has surprised me with this move. I underestimated him." Kuuitsi spread his hands, drawing a few smiles as he played to the crowd. "I don't say that often," he said. "Certainly not where Akik is concerned. But make no mistake," he said, changing his tone to deliver a carefully pitched warning, "this changes things." He gestured at Gaba and the small but capable SRU team. "What started as an unusual hustle..." Kuuitsi paused as he reflected on his choice of words. "I think that's right. It was a hustle."

He paused again to nod at Maratse as he entered the briefing room, waited for him to take a seat, and then continued.

"Akik had a wonderful idea, and he wanted to show off. That's my take on the situation – Akik's hustle. He hassled a visiting American, a tourist. And if that had been that, then we wouldn't be here now. At least," he said, with another glance at Gaba. "Not in such force. But the situation has changed. These men," he said, jerking his thumb over his shoulder at the screen behind him, "have seen to that. Their names are Michael Potter..." Kuuitsi glanced at the screen, adding, "The taller of the two. And James Marshall. Forty-six, and thirty-three years old. Potter is unknown to us. But Marshall's name popped up on Interpol with a prior history, including a short stint in a Swedish jail on drug-related charges. He was released and returned to the US authorities, with whom we believe he cooperated. His sentence was reduced for good behaviour." Kuuitsi paused again. "I think we can agree," he said, another pause, and a glance at Maratse. "It is unlikely either of these men intends to behave. In fact, it's my guess that Marshall, at least, has been sent to Greenland to misbehave to make up for his sins of cooperation."

Gaba shuffled his feet, drawing Kuuitsi's attention.

"We're going to let him," the commissioner said, following his cue from Kuuitsi. He stood up, walked to the podium, and addressed the room as Kuuitsi stepped to one side. "We're tracking Potter and Marshall and expect them to arrive by fishing trawler in Nuuk sometime early tomorrow morning. Those of you who drew the short straw will be covering the docks through the night. Plain clothes. Observation only. Be discreet," the commissioner said. He nodded at Gaba. "Sergeant?"

"SRU has tactical command," Gaba said, taking a step away from the wall. "No one pulls a weapon without my authority. The likelihood of these men being armed with anything other than a knife is low." He paused to look at Maratse, and then added, "Although it's not impossible they have a sawed-off shotgun. We're going to assume as much." Another glance at Maratse. "Everyone should assume that. But not everyone is going to get close. SRU is on point. Everyone else will go about their usual business, stick to your normal patrols, but stay alert."

"Questions?" the commissioner said. He pointed at a female officer in the second row. "Yes?"

"Are these men coming to meet Akik?"

The commissioner nodded, letting Kuuitsi answer the question.

"*Aap*. We believe the meet should have taken place in Copenhagen. But for some reason, Akik convinced them to come here."

"And Akik?" the officer said. "I thought he was meeting the American?" She paused before adding, "For the side hustle."

"Side hustle." Kuuitsi grinned. "I like that. *Aap*," he said. "We now believe the stamps and the cachets Mr Bennett has drawn for them are a distraction. But Akik, bless him..." Kuuitsi paused for a round of soft laughter and discreet chuckles. "Still wants to meet. He's reached out. Mr Bennett will meet with Akik in the foyer of *Katuaq* tomorrow morning at nine. Constable Maratse will accompany Mr Bennett. They will both be wearing a wire."

"A wire?" the commissioner asked, playing the innocent stooge once more.

"*Aap*," Kuuitsi said. He turned to the room before answering the commissioner's question. "This *side hustle* is the excuse to meet, and *our* excuse to come out of the shadows and reveal to Akik that we know exactly what's going on. Of course, with Constable Maratse's little sideshow earlier today..." Kuuitsi paused as the officers turned their heads to look at Maratse. "We've already played our hand. Akik knows we know. Mr Bennett has agreed to play his part, and in doing so, we'll find out what Akik really wants." Kuuitsi pointed at the two white men on the screen. "It's just possible Akik wants to trade these men for something, but if he does, then it's news to me." Kuuitsi offered the commissioner an apologetic shrug. "My sources have failed me on this one," he said.

"Which is why we're entertaining this little charade in the first place," the commissioner said. He straightened his back, then turned to look at the rows of men and women, twenty officers, not counting the team of four SRU officers, Kuuitsi and himself. "Don't be fooled by Akik's novel idea with the stamps and the cachets. There's something else at play here, and don't forget," he said, turning to catch Maratse's eye, "there's a girl involved in this. Her safety, and Mr Bennett's safety, are your top priority. Gaba is calling the shots, but I want you visible when you need to be. The meeting at *Katuaq* will be a busy one. It's day two of the stamp convention." The commissioner sighed and said, "Akik might not be the smartest tool in the box, but he knows how to pick his venues. Be diligent," the commissioner said. "And get a good night's rest."

The commissioner added the last comment for Maratse's benefit, but he was already gone, slipping out of the door before Gaba could stop him.

Part 8

Sergeant Kuuitsi shared the latest update from the plain-clothes unit shadowing the Americans since their arrival in Nuuk, confirming that Potter and Marshall had arrived, that they appeared *sleepy but motivated* as the constables described them, but unarmed. "To the best of our knowledge," Kuuitsi said.

Kuuitsi smiled as the SRU promptly ignored the last bit of information and continued to prepare their gear as if they were going to war. Maratse watched from the opposite side of the ready room, grunting as a technician attached the microphone inside the collar of Maratse's jacket, and again when the technician enquired if Maratse had considered washing the jacket.

"*Eeqqi*," Maratse said, nodding curtly when the technician was finished. He looked up as Juulia entered the room.

"He's all set," she said, jerking her thumb at Dave as a second technician tucked the wires of Dave's microphone out of sight. "A little nervous, but all right."

"Hmm," Maratse said. He watched Juulia as she zipped her jacket to her chin and clapped her arms across her chest. A thin trickle of sweat rolled down the back of Maratse's neck and he gave Juulia a second look. "How about you?" he asked.

"Me?" Juulia's eyes widened for a second before she shook her head. "I'm fine. All good. Ready to go."

"And you have your phone?"

"My phone?"

Maratse nodded.

"Sure," Juulia said. She frowned as she pulled it out of her pocket, and again when she tried to hand it to Maratse. He pressed his finger to his lips instead, then guided Juulia to the corner of the room with a light touch of her elbow.

Maratse curled his fist around the tiny mic attached to his collar and said, "Map."

"What?"

"Open it," he whispered.

Juulia swiped the map onto the screen, and then pointed at the GPS marker showing their location inside the police station, just a short walk from *Katuaq*.

"Meet me here," Maratse said, tapping a cracked and dirty nail on the far side of the cultural centre. "Back door," he whispered. "Twenty minutes."

"On foot?" Juulia said, frowning.

Maratse shook his head, and said, "Patrol car."

"Got it," Juulia said, although the crease on her brow suggested she wouldn't really *get it* until she met Maratse twenty minutes later. She slipped her phone back into her pocket as Gaba called the room to order.

"Plain-clothes are trailing the Americans," he said, adding, "The *new* Americans." Gaba switched to English. "If you're ready, Mr Bennett."

"I am."

"Then Constable Maratse will walk you over to the centre. We have officers inside. You are completely safe. And, as you can see, Maratse has dressed for the occasion."

Two of the SRU officers smirked as Gaba gestured at Maratse's uniform, with a nod at the pistol holstered at Maratse's hip.

"This is no longer a covert operation," Gaba said. "If it ever was. Akik is expecting us. He's expecting *him*," he said, with another nod at Maratse. "Everything is going to plan, and Sergeant Kuuitsi here…" Gaba paused as Kuuitsi raised his hand.

"Present," he said, drawing another round of smirks and giggles, including Juulia, until she caught Maratse's eye. She tucked her hands into her pockets as Gaba continued.

"Synchronise your watches," he said, waiting for everyone to do so. "Maratse?"

"Hmm," Maratse said. He rolled back his sleeves.

Gaba sighed and removed a heavy watch from his wrist. He walked across the room, slapped it into Maratse's hand, and then pulled a spare watch from the front pocket of his ballistic vest. Gaba attached it to the shoulder strap of his vest, waited for Maratse to put his watch on, and then snapped his fingers.

"Go," he said, and ushered everyone out of the room.

"Stick with Maratse," Juulia said as she walked alongside Dave. "He'll look after you."

"Yes," Dave said.

Juulia kept the conversation going to the front door of the police station, and then stopped as Dave took a long deep breath of chill late April air.

"I expected more snow," he said.

"Up north." Maratse pointed.

"And sea ice?"

"*Iiji.*"

"Ah, *yes*," Dave said and smiled. "I'm getting the hang of it. But no ice here?" He turned east as if to look out to sea.

"Too warm," Maratse said. "But the lakes are frozen."

"What lakes?"

"Small ones," Maratse said. "In the mountains." Maratse pointed again, directing Dave's gaze to the large mountain just beyond the city. "Ukkusissat," he said. "The Danes call it…"

"Store Malene," Gaba said, interrupting. He tapped the watch on his vest. "Time to go."

Maratse looked at Juulia, waited a beat for her to dip her head – the briefest of nods – and then gestured to Dave that they should start walking. Dave adjusted his satchel and patted the front pocket. He talked as they walked, leaving Gaba and the SRU in the parking area outside the police station. The gravel crunched under their feet. The hard-packed snow squealed beneath their soles. Dave patted the pocket again.

"I must have checked it one hundred times already," he said. "The cachets are there. I *know* they are. It's silly. I'm just…"

"Nervous," Maratse said as they approached the

entrance to *Katuaq*.

"Yes, exactly." Dave pressed his hand on Maratse's arm as he reached for the door. "And you, Constable? Are you nervous?"

Maratse shrugged, and said, "Not nervous."

"No?"

"Committed," Maratse said. He opened the door.

Dave followed Maratse inside, bumping shoulders with familiar faces, smiling when someone recognised him, slowing when they reached out to shake his hand, only to apologise as Maratse took his elbow and guided him away and through the busy foyer. Dave spotted Akik before Maratse did and slowed as the all too familiar scar on Akik's chin agitated the flock of imaginary geese inside Dave's stomach.

"He's there," he whispered.

Maratse looked up, caught Akik's eye, and then promptly pulled Dave towards the toilets.

"But he's right *there*," Dave said as Maratse opened the door, pushing him inside. "I thought…"

Dave stopped thinking as Maratse tugged at Dave's shirttails, pulling them out of his jeans and pressing his hands into the small of Dave's back. Dave opened his mouth to speak, but Maratse silenced him with a look. Maratse said nothing for a few seconds, and then, a small plastic *snap* and a second later, he placed the microphone unit in Dave's hand before pulling the mic itself from Dave's collar. Maratse pressed his finger to his lips, silencing Dave for a second time as he removed his own microphone. He bundled the two units together, stuffed them into the cargo pocket of his trousers, and then checked the cubicles. Satisfied they were alone, Maratse locked the toilet door.

"Restroom scene," Maratse said, and leaned against the counter.

"What?"

Maratse added a brief smile to put Dave at ease, and said, "I'm learning."

"Yes…" Dave said.

"This," Maratse gestured at the room, "is private." He tapped his trouser pocket. "Just you, me, and Akik."

"I'm not sure I understand," Dave said.

"You don't need to." Maratse pushed away from the counter, collecting Dave on his way to the door with another gentle pinch of the American's elbow. "Just listen," he said. "You're my witness."

"Okay." Dave took a breath as Maratse opened the door. He held it all the way to Akik. Maratse prompted him to breathe with a tap of the arm, before reaching out to shake Akik's hand. The Greenlander with the scarred chin glanced at Dave and then turned his attention to Maratse.

"Tiilla said you chased her," he said in English.

"I did."

"To get to me?"

"To get to Tiilla."

Akik cupped his chin in his hand, ignoring the press of people around them. He glanced a couple of times at two men, turning Maratse's head. He grinned when Maratse nodded, confirming they were who Akik thought they were.

"Police," Akik said.

"*Iiji.*"

"For me?"

"*Imaqa*," Maratse said. "Maybe."

Akik switched to Greenlandic and said, "Or maybe for my friends?"

"Friends?" Maratse said, ignoring the frown on Dave's brow as he continued in Greenlandic. "Can you trust them?"

"*Naamik*," Akik said. "But they pay well." He grinned again and said, "They paid well for you."

"Hmm," Maratse said.

Akik waited a beat and then leaned in close to whisper to Maratse. "I have a daughter. Nauja is sick. I want to take her to Disneyland, you know?"

"*Iiji*," Maratse said.

"I thought so." Akik pulled back. "I thought you would understand."

"What about Tiilla?"

"She stays with me until you come to meet with my friends."

Maratse nodded, and then said, "I decide where we meet."

"Sure."

"I decide when."

Akik shook his head. "One hour from now. As soon as they lose their tail."

Maratse turned his head to catch the eye of a plain-clothes police officer tapping his ear as he walked past.

"Problem?" Akik said, once the officer had moved on.

"No problem," Maratse said. He checked Gaba's watch on his wrist, tapped the screen above the minute hand, and said, "On the reservoir. In one hour."

"On?" Akik said, tilting his head as he queried Maratse.

"*Iiji*," Maratse said. "In the middle."

Akik nodded. "One hour," he said, and turned away.

"Ah, just a second," Dave said as he opened the front pocket of his satchel. "You wanted these. Didn't you?"

Akik smiled and then pointed at Maratse. "I have no more need for them." He walked away, disappearing into the crowd as Dave shot a quizzical look at Maratse.

"I don't understand."

"Tiilla," Maratse said.

"The girl?"

"*Iiji.*"

"You said…"

"It was always about the girl," Maratse said. "And who she knew."

"She knows you," Dave said.

"She does."

Dave grasped the cachets in both hands as he thought it through. "He pointed at you."

"*Iiji.*"

"Then it's you he wants." Dave laughed, then clapped his hand to his mouth. "I'm so sorry. I thought it was about me. How silly."

"Not silly," Maratse said. He took Dave's arm and led him through the crowd to a small table where a woman sat and beckoned to them.

"Qilaatti," Dave said, and she smiled.

"You remembered."

"Yes, of course." Dave turned to Maratse. He held up the cachets, smiling as Qilaatti cast a hungry eye at them. "Do we need these?"

"*Eeqqi*," Maratse said.

"Ah, that means *no*." Dave grinned and turned to Qilaatti. "I've learned Greenlandic since we last met."

"East Greenlandic," she said.

"Well, yes." Dave gave a theatrical sigh, adding, "One language, so many dialects…"

"And new cachets," Qilaatti said. "May I see them?"

"You can have them," Dave said. "To make up for our spoiled dinner plans." He pressed the cachets into Qilaatti's hand, and then turned as Maratse walked away from the table. Dave excused himself, promising to return *in a second*, as Qilaatti examined his artwork. "Constable?" he said, thrusting out his hand as Maratse turned. "I wanted to thank you for looking after me," he said.

Maratse took Dave's hand and nodded.

"You're a man of few words, Constable," Dave said. "But perhaps a few of my own would suffice." He smiled as the word *suffice* furrowed Maratse's brow. "It has been a pleasure, Constable."

"*Iiji.*"

"And if we should ever meet again, perhaps we could have another coffee, or maybe even four espressos." Dave grinned. "Whatever you like."

"I would like that," Maratse said. He pulled back his sleeve and looked at Gaba's watch.

"But you have to go," Dave said. "I'm sorry.

Don't let me keep you, wherever it is you are going."

"To get Tiilla," Maratse said. "To take her home."

"Yes," Dave said. "I understand."

Dave offered his hand again, wincing slightly as Maratse gave him a hunter's grip, and then watched as Maratse turned to weave his way through the crowd. He lost sight of him as Maratse approached the fire exit, but a flurry of police officers parting the convention crowd in pursuit gave him a final glimpse as the constable in the dirty jacket left the building.

"Barely in uniform," Dave said, before turning back to Qilaatti as she haggled the price of exclusive cachets with a group of enthusiastic stamp collectors.

Part 9

Constable Juulia Piaraq bumped the police patrol car over the curb and charged across the snow-pocked gravel behind *Katuaq*. She stomped on the brakes as Maratse burst out of the fire door, only to accelerate as he urged her forward with exaggerated waves. He leaped onto the running board and grabbed the rails on the roof as Juulia sped away from the cultural centre. Maratse slapped his hand on the roof for her to stop when they reached the road and then jogged around the front of the car to climb into the passenger seat.

"Drive," he said, as soon as he got into the car.

Juulia clutched the steering wheel. She stared straight ahead.

"Constable?"

"*Aap?*" Juulia said. She kept her eyes fixed straight ahead.

"I said drive."

"I know."

Juulia looked over her shoulder at the three plain-clothes police officers running towards them.

"We have to go," Maratse said.

He leaned forward to turn on the siren, jolting Juulia out of her thoughts and back into action. She jerked the gearstick into first and thumped her foot on the accelerator pedal.

"Left," Maratse said when they reached the

main road, and then, "Right," when they got to the T junction joining *H.J. Rinkip Aqqutaa.*

"Where are we going?"

"Qinngorput," Maratse said.

Juulia accelerated into a gap in traffic, and then flinched as Gaba's voice burst out of the radio speakers mounted on the dash. Maratse turned him off.

"I need to be at the reservoir in forty-seven minutes," Maratse said.

"Why?"

"To get Tiilla." Maratse tapped Juulia's knee as she lifted her foot slightly off the accelerator. "Keep going," he said. "We need to take a roundabout route."

"Why?"

"Gaba is coming."

Juulia swallowed, gripped the wheel, and then accelerated. Maratse encouraged her to change gear, then said nothing, letting her drive. He grabbed the handle above the door, holding on as Juulia weaved in and out of traffic. The siren cleared the way, and Maratse reached out to turn on the emergency lights. He allowed himself a small grin and then pointed at the first roundabout on the road to Qinngorput.

"Left and into the second housing area."

Juulia nodded. Maratse killed the lights and siren.

"Slow down," he said.

Juulia parked on the drive of the second house on a crescent-shaped street, shooting confused looks at Maratse as he pressed his head to the glass and looked out of the passenger window. She opened her mouth to speak, but Maratse beat her to it.

"There's a mole in the police department," he said. "I think that's the word. Traitor, maybe."

"A traitor?" Juulia shook her head and said, "I don't understand."

"Someone is taking money from the Americans."

"The government?"

"*Eeqqi*," Maratse said. He looked at Juulia. "Organised crime."

"And what has this got to do with you?"

Maratse paused as a police car raced past them on the main street, before adding, "I killed some men once. It was in Uummannaq. I was alone. Tiilla and Katu were in trouble. I made sure trouble left them alone."

"And now?"

Maratse sighed as he looked at Juulia. "It came back. Caught up with us, with Tiilla."

"And the mole?"

"Made sure I was the only officer in Uummannaq. They cleared the way for a light plane with extra fuel tanks to cross Greenland." Maratse flattened his lips into a thin smile as he remembered the plane, the fuel tanks, and a fiery young aircraft mechanic called Piipa Kajussen.

"You killed the pilot?"

"I killed the men who came looking for him. The pilot was already dead."

"I don't understand," Juulia said.

"It doesn't matter."

Maratse looked at Gaba's watch, admired it for

a moment, and then pulled out the crown to adjust the time. He took the watch off and gave it to Juulia.

"Gaba is coming. Give him the watch. Tell him I've synchronised it." Maratse smiled as Juulia stared at the watch. "At that time," he said, tapping the watch face, "Gaba should be in position."

"To do what?"

"To stop the mole."

"And me?" Juulia slipped the watch into her pocket. "What will I be doing?"

"Driving as fast as you can up the hill to the reservoir."

"What?"

Maratse opened the door and slipped one leg off the chair, ready to climb out of the patrol car. "Keep your speed up, but slow down just before the top. Otherwise…" Maratse drew an exaggerated arc in the air with a curved hand. Juulia swallowed.

"And now?" she asked. "What do I do now?"

Maratse looked over his shoulder as a bright yellow bus drove slowly up the hill. The name *Qinngorput* flashed across the sign above the driver, and Maratse got ready to run.

"Find Gaba," he said. "Give him the watch."

Juulia leaned over the passenger seat as Maratse ran for the bus. She called out, "How do you know the mole will be there?" But Maratse was already gone.

Maratse tucked himself into a seat at the back of the bus. The journey ate away another twenty minutes as the bus stopped and started slowing for traffic, before taking a detour to the airport and back. Maratse pushed the stop button as they reached Qinngorput, congratulating himself as he remembered to get off at the stop just before the wide gravel track leading up to the reservoir at the top. He tightened his utility belt, adjusted his jacket, and then stooped to tie his bootlaces before beginning the short climb to the reservoir. Maratse slowed as he reached the top, took a good look around the frozen body of water, studying the shadows behind boulders, and then walked onto the ice. Maratse walked out to the centre of the reservoir and stopped. He lit a cigarette, clamped it between his lips, and stuffed his hands into his jacket pockets as he smoked.

A curious raven cawed and croaked from its perch to Maratse's right. Maratse studied it, picturing the thick brush of hairs around the raven's beak – a fine detail, too far away to see, but something Maratse was fascinated by as a child. Ravens were part of the land, year-round, living and breeding in the harshest of conditions, just like the Greenlanders.

Living and breeding.

The thought made Maratse smile.

He finished one cigarette, adjusted his collar in the thin wind, and then lit another. He had smoked half before the sound of a vehicle labouring up the track turned his head. He watched the SUV as the driver parked to one side. He held his breath as the doors opened. Two white men got out of the back. Maratse guessed they were the Americans. He recognised the driver and watched Akik as he walked to the rear of the vehicle. Akik popped the rear door and reached inside to pull Tiilla out of the boot. The fourth man wore a police uniform. He pulled at the hem of his jacket as if to straighten it, and then gave up, preferring the casual look. It took another minute before the police officer was close enough for Maratse to recognise him.

"Constable Maratse," Sergeant Iaaku Kuuitsi said. "This is unexpected."

"Hmm," Maratse said. He took his hands out of his pockets. His right strayed towards the pistol on his belt, only to stop when Kuuitsi drew his pistol and pointed it at Maratse.

"Take it out slowly, Constable," he said in English. "And then take it apart."

"I'll take it," said the taller of the two Americans.

Potter, Maratse remembered, as he thought back to Kuuitsi's briefing.

"That's all right, Potter," Kuuitsi said. "It's enough to disarm him, right?"

"To begin with," Potter said.

Maratse removed his pistol and scattered the magazine and the parts on the ice. He switched his gaze from Kuuitsi and the Americans for a moment to look at Tiilla.

"Are you all right?" he asked in Greenlandic.

She nodded.

"I've come to take you home," Maratse said.

Tiilla nodded again and then shrank into Akik's side as Kuuitsi raised his pistol.

"It was very clever of you to get rid of the mic," he said, taking a step closer to Maratse. "The only people who knew where to meet were…"

"Akik," Maratse said, with a nod at the scarred man. "Me."

"And the mole, once Akik told him." Kuuitsi laughed. "How clever you have been. And to think I underestimated you."

"Speak English, for God's sake," Potter said. "We're paying you enough."

"Of course." Kuuitsi nodded. "My apologies."

"Accepted," Potter said. "Now get on with it."

Maratse looked at the Americans and then nodded as he realised why they had come.

"You're here to watch," he said. "To report back."

"That's right," Marshall said, taking over from his partner. "We paid a lot of money for the sergeant to smooth our way. He failed."

"That's not quite right," Kuuitsi said. He lowered the pistol a little as the American pointed at Maratse.

"You were supposed to remove any and *all* problems." He stabbed a finger at Maratse, parting the clouds of breath misting out of his mouth. "You didn't."

"Your plane was supposed to fly straight over Greenland," Kuuitsi said. It was his turn to point at Maratse. "It didn't. And then he happened."

"And now you put it right," Marshall said. "An eye for an eye."

"You really expect me to shoot a fellow police officer?"

Kuuitsi waited for Marshall to respond, but silence was the American's only answer.

Maratse lit his third cigarette.

"We'll let him smoke," Kuuitsi said. "Just a few puffs."

The Americans shuffled on the ice, cursing the thin soles of their shoes as they waited. The raven croaked, filling the shallow basin of rock walls, cupping the reservoir with its harsh echo. Maratse watched it take flight and then wondered if Gaba had gotten the message. Had Gaba spooked the raven? And what *steps* had Gaba taken?

Maratse looked at the pistol in Kuuitsi's hand.

"That's not a service pistol," he said.

Kuuitsi looked at the pistol and turned it in the light. "I can't shoot you with my service pistol, Constable. So I asked our mutual friend for some assistance." Kuuitsi shrugged and said, "This is what he had available." Kuuitsi raised the pistol, said something about the weight, and then applied a little more pressure on the trigger.

"Do it," Potter said, but his words were lost in the growl of a vehicle roaring up the track. Kuuitsi turned just as a dark blue police patrol car burst over the lip of the track and described a perfect arc in the air, not unlike the arc Maratse had drawn with his hand.

"Jesus!" Potter said, as the patrol car slammed onto the short stretch of gravel between the top of the track and the reservoir. The rear door swung open as the car bounced, just as Juulia Piaraq stuffed her foot on the accelerator and launched onto the ice.

A single rifle shot rang out from rocks on Maratse's right, about twenty metres from the spot where the raven had perched. The bullet clipped Kuuitsi's shoulder, spinning him onto the ice. The sergeant squeezed the pistol trigger twice in Maratse's direction. Maratse clutched his stomach in anticipation of the bullets puncturing his belly, only to frown as Kuuitsi fired again.

"Damn you, Gaba!" Kuuitsi tossed the pistol onto the ice, then shouted at the Americans to, "Leave it. It's full of blanks."

Tiilla stomped the side of her boot down Akik's shin and then ran towards Maratse. She screamed as the patrol car spun on the ice, turning wide circles, clipping Marshall with the front of the vehicle, just as Maratse scooped Tiilla into his arms. The patrol car slid past them, and Maratse ran after it. He reached out for the door handle and held on, sliding as the car spun a fourth circle on the ice. Tiilla screamed again as the door closed, threatening to pinch her and Maratse, but Maratse elbowed it open, stuffed Tiilla into the boot, and shouted at Juulia.

"Drive!"

Maratse closed the rear door as Juulia stuffed the patrol car into first. The car slid to a stop and Juulia teased it across the ice until she had enough momentum to accelerate, heading for the track at the opposite end of the reservoir. Maratse watched them go, and then waved at Gaba and the three SRU officers as they jogged across the ice towards him.

"Constable," Gaba roared once his men had secured Kuuitsi and the Americans. "If you ever pull a stunt like that again…"

Maratse held up his hands to ward off Gaba's

wrath, only to lower them again as Gaba came closer.

"Me?" he said.

"*Aap,*" Gaba said, spit flecking his bottom lip as he spat to one side. "Everything was under control until *you* showed up, Constable. I had taken…"

"Steps." Maratse nodded. "I know. *Qujanaq.*"

Gaba stopped, and then said, "Sure. Fine. You're welcome."

"But," Maratse said, with a nod at Kuuitsi and the SRU man tending to the bullet wound in the sergeant's shoulder. "It means you knew."

"I had suspicions," Gaba said. "I didn't *know.*"

"Hmm," Maratse said.

Gaba snorted. "Okay, Constable. Maybe I *did* know. Maybe a little."

The SRU sergeant paused before continuing, but Maratse had moved on. He thought of Juulia driving Tiilla back to the station, and then one step further as he imagined taking her with him back to Uummannaq.

"Constable?" Gaba said.

Maratse looked up.

"Are you listening?"

"*Imaqa,*" Maratse said. "Maybe."

Part 10

Tiilla Tinnaaq thumped her good leg against the side of the desk as Juulia plied her with fizzy drinks, bars of chocolate, and anything else she considered was necessary when dealing with shock. The desk was an awkward affair, tucked beneath a set of wooden stairs leading to a tiny room with a locked door. Juulia wondered about its position as the commissioner, Gaba, and Maratse had each deposited a generous amount of dust and grit on the surface of the desk when they climbed the stairs. Juulia brushed it to one side, gave Tiilla another bar of chocolate, and treated herself to a can of cola. She leaned back in the chair and tilted her head to one side in the hope of catching more of the hushed conversation leaking out of the room at the top of the stairs.

Maratse leaned against the wall as Gaba briefed the commissioner on the events that had occurred on the ice.

"That's not what worries me," the commissioner said. "The actions on the reservoir were contained. No tourists." He glanced at Maratse. "That part of your plan, at least, was smart, Constable."

"*Iiji*," Maratse said.

"The rest of it, however…"

Gaba interrupted the commissioner with a

cough, and said, "To be fair, Commissioner, we're the ones who dragged Maratse into this. I think the best we can do, once he's written his report, is send him up north."

"Sergeant?"

"I know," Gaba said. He smoothed his hand over his shaved head, adding, "It's not like me to take Maratse's side, but…"

"You're going soft, Sergeant."

"Maybe I am, sir."

The commissioner laughed and said, "It suits you." He turned to Maratse. "There's a plane tomorrow morning. Gaba tells me you intend to take Tiilla back to Uummannaq."

"*Iiji,*" Maratse said.

"But I thought her family was dead?"

"They are, sir," Gaba said. "But Maratse has a plan."

"You do?"

Maratse nodded.

"And it's better than the last one?"

"*Iiji,*" Maratse said.

"Then go ahead, Constable. Gaba and I will deal with the Americans, Akik, and the fallout around Sergeant Kuuitsi. It is, as Gaba says, our problem."

Maratse left them to it, unlocked the door, and tramped down the stairs, spilling more grit onto the poorly positioned desk.

"I don't know who sits at this desk," Juulia said, wiping Maratse's grit onto the floor. "But they should think about moving somewhere else – *anywhere* else."

"Hmm," Maratse said. He cast a casual eye over the desk, lingered over the neat handwriting and stack of notebooks arranged as far from the stairs as possible, and smiled. "I have an idea who it might be," he said.

Maratse nodded at Tiilla and then held out his hand. She grasped his fingers, and he tugged her off the desk. Tiilla thumped onto the floor, then pulled free of Maratse to wrap her arms around Juulia. Maratse waited, fidgeted for a moment, and then moved to one side as Tiilla let go of Juulia and headed to the door.

"You'll have to visit," he said, as Juulia stood up.

"Maybe I will. If I don't get fired."

"Fired?" Maratse frowned. "Why?"

"The driving," Juulia said, lowering her voice to a whisper. "Remember, I had a dispensation? Sergeant Gaba saw me come over the top of the hill. He *saw* me. And you told me I had to take the speed off before the top."

"*Iiji,*" Maratse said.

"I know, but I didn't. And now…" Juulia glanced up at the room at the top of the stairs. "What will Gaba say to the commissioner?"

Maratse offered Juulia his hand, smiled when she shook it, and said, "He'll say it was the best driving he has ever seen."

"Really?"

Maratse nodded, safe in the assumption that if Sergeant Gaba Alatak could look through his fingers at Maratse's list of indiscretions, Juulia's adrenalin-fuelled driving techniques were low on the list of punishable actions.

"You'll be fine," he said, followed by, "*Qujanaq.*"

Maratse left Juulia at the foot of the stairs and then followed Tiilla out of the police station.

Tiilla spent her last night in Nuuk at the Children's Home, introducing Maratse to all the children before the adults on shift rescued him, gave him a room in the staff section, and promised a hearty breakfast before they flew north the following morning.

Maratse settled on a simple, but strong coffee for breakfast, taking it in the recreation room while Tiilla said her last goodbyes. He crouched in front of a small, neglected bookshelf and plucked an almost pristine copy of a Philip K. Dick science fiction book off the shelf. He finished his coffee and promised to return the book the next time he was in Nuuk.

"Keep it," said the head of the home. "The kids aren't interested."

"Hmm," Maratse said. "*Qujanaq.*"

He tucked the book into his jacket pocket and then helped Tiilla carry her things to the taxi. They were airborne forty-minutes later.

"Where am I going to stay?" Tiilla asked as they landed in Qaarsut.

"With a friend," Maratse said.

"Your friend?"

"*Iiji.*"

"Will I go to school?"

95

Maratse nodded. "*Iiji*," he said, followed by, "Every day," when Tiilla stuck out her bottom lip. He tapped her arm as the helicopter landed in front of the airport building and then gathered their things.

The helicopter flew low over the sea ice. Tiilla sat close to the window, tapping Maratse's arm and pointing at the houses she knew, the cars she recognised, the clumps of sledge dogs lounging on the icy rocks, and the big teams racing across the sea ice, heading for home. They landed shortly after, gathered Tiilla's small collection of bags, and then bundled out of the heliport building and into the patrol car. Constable Aqqa Danielsen grasped Maratse's hand in a tight grip once the luggage was secured in the boot.

"Thank God you came back," he said. "It's been non-stop since you left.

Maratse grinned and climbed into the passenger seat.

Aqqa drove at a leisurely pace through town, stopping each time Tiilla saw someone she knew. They waited for Tiilla to greet children of all ages, and adults who knew her family, knew the story, but almost couldn't recognise her now that she had grown.

"It's only been a couple of years," Tiilla said as she climbed back into the patrol car.

The last stop was a small wooden house with white walls and a black roof overlooking the frozen fjord. The dogs tethered to the rocks at the end of long chains looked up with casual interest as Maratse got out of the patrol car. He stooped to fuss over those that were closest, and then stood up as the door opened and Seeri Asasaq stepped out onto her porch.

"Constable Maratse," she said. "Have you come back to pay off your debt?"

"*Iiji*," he said with a dip of his head. "And I brought a friend."

Maratse gestured for Tiilla to go on ahead as he grabbed her bags, smiling as the words *hot chocolate* and *tell me all about it* drifted out of the door, over the wooden deck, and across the icy rocks to Maratse. He lit a cigarette, nodded when Aqqa suggested he pick him up later, and looked out over the sea ice at the crooked tip on the summit of Qilertinnguit in the distance. Seeri's lead dog bumped its side against Maratse's leg, as if to remind him that everything was going to be all right.

"*Iiji*," he said, reaching down to fuss over the dog's ears. "Everything's going to be fine."

The End

About the Author

Christoffer Petersen is the author's pen name. He lives in Denmark. Chris started writing stories about Greenland while teaching in Qaanaaq, the largest village in the very north of Greenland – the population peaked at 600 during the two years he lived there. Chris spent a total of seven years in Greenland, teaching in remote communities and at the Police Academy in the capital of Nuuk.

Chris continues to be inspired by the vast icy wilderness of the Arctic and his books have a common setting in the region, with a Scandinavian influence. He has also watched enough Bourne movies to no longer be surprised by the plot, but not enough to get bored.

You can find Chris in Denmark or online here:

www.christoffer-petersen.com

By the same Author

CHRISTOFFER PETERSEN

BAIT
THE WOMEN'S KNIFE
ICE, WIND & FIRE
THE AMERICAN ARTISAN
OF DOGS AND MEN

THE GREENLAND TRILOGY
featuring Konstabel Fenna Brongaard
THE ICE STAR
IN THE SHADOW OF THE MOUNTAIN
THE SHAMAN'S HOUSE

THE DARK ADVENT SERIES
featuring Police Commissioner
Petra "Piitalaat" Jensen
THE CALENDAR MAN
THE TWELFTH NIGHT
INVISIBLE TOUCH
NORTH STAR BAY

THE POLARPOL ACTION THRILLERS
featuring Sergeant Petra "Piitalaat" Jensen
and more
NORTHERN LIGHT
MOUNTAIN GHOST

UNDERCOVER GREENLAND
introducing Inniki Rasmussen *and* Eko Simigaq
NARKOTIKA

THE DETECTIVE FREJA HANSEN SERIES
set in Denmark and Scotland
FELL RUNNER Introductory novella

BLACKOUT INGÉNUE

MADE IN DENMARK
short stories featuring Milla Moth *set in Denmark*
DANISH DESIGN

THE WHEELMAN SHORTS
short stories featuring Noah Lee *set in Australia*
PULP DRIVER

THE WILD CRIME SERIES
featuring wildlife biologist Jon Østergård
set in Denmark and Alaska
PAINT THE DEVIL
LOST IN THE WOODS
CHERNOBYL WOLVES

GREENLAND NOIR (POETRY)
inspired by Seven Graves, One Winter & more
GREENLAND NOIR Volume 1

GUERRILLA GREENLAND
featuring Constable David Maratse
ARCTIC STATE
ARCTIC REBEL
ARCTIC RISING
ARCTIC RECOIL

THE GREENLAND MISSING PERSONS SERIES
featuring Constable Petra "Piitalaat" Jensen
THE BOY WITH THE NARWHAL TOOTH
THE GIRL WITH THE RAVEN TONGUE
THE SHIVER IN THE ARCTIC

CHRISTOFFER PETERSEN

THE FEVER IN THE WATER
THE WINTER TRAP
THE SHAMAN'S DAUGHTER
THE BANSHEE PALACE
THE ICE WHISPERS
THE BLOOD BANDIT
THE ROCK THIEF
THE GLACIER WRAITH
THE BLISTER AT THE END OF THE WORLD
THE BOREAL TATTOO

Made in the USA
Las Vegas, NV
07 November 2022

58979825R00062